Dictionary of
Financial Abbreviations

Dictionary of Financial Abbreviations

John Paxton

FITZROY DEARBORN
An Imprint of the Taylor and Francis Group
New York • London

Published in 2003 by
Fitzroy Dearborn
An Imprint of the Taylor and Francis Group
29 West 35th Street
New York, NY 10001

Published in Great Britain by
Fitzroy Dearborn
An Imprint of the Taylor and Francis Group
11 New Fetter Lane
London EC4P 4EE

10 9 8 7 6 5 4 3 2

British Library and Library of Congress Cataloging-in-Publication Data are available.

Typeset by Alacrity, Banwell Castle, Weston-super-Mare.
Printed in the United States of America on acid-free paper.

ISBN 1-57958-397-0

Contents

for

DIONE DAFFIN

A great helper over the years

on many books

Acknowledgements

I HAVE BEEN GIVEN great help by several hundred banks, libraries, embassies, high commissions, and professional and regulatory organizations, for which I am very grateful, but should like to thank the following for exceptional help:

London Stock Exchange, London Metal Exchange, Chartered Institute of Personnel and Development, Institute of Chartered Secretaries and Administrators, Association of Average Adjusters, Chartered Institute of Loss Adjusters, Association of Accounting Technicians, Association of Business Recovery Professionals, Association of Chartered Certified Accountants, Association of Corporate Treasurers, British Association of Communicators in Business, British Computer Society, Building Societies Association, Chartered Institute of Bankers in Scotland, National Association of Realtors, National Futures Association, European Central Bank, Financial Accounting Standards Board, Council of Mortgage Lenders, Financial Ombudsman Service, Pensions Ombudsman, PIA Ombudsman Bureau, Association of Private Client Investment Managers and Stockbrokers, ProShare, Department of Trade and Industry (UK), Insolvency Service, Bank of England, Board of Inland Revenue, Building Societies Commission, Competition Commission, Export Credits Guarantee Department (UK), National Audit Office, National Investment and Loans Office, Royal Mint, Chartered Institute of Public Finance and Accountancy, Institute of Administrative Management, Institute of Chartered Accountants in England and Wales, Institute of Export, Lloyd's Register of Shipping, Financial Services Authority, Consultative Committee of Accountancy Bodies, Finance and Leasing Association, American Institute of Certified Public Accountants, Governmental Accounting Standards Board, International Accounting Standards Committee, International Federation of Accountants, London Library, Institute of Company Accountants, British Airports Authority, Institute of Management, City Business Library (London), Danish Bankers' Association, Financial Accounting Federation, and the International Securities Market Association.

The following embassies and high commissions in the United Kingdom have also been helpful: Australian High Commission, Embassy of Belgium, Canadian High Commission, Royal Danish Embassy, Embassy of Finland, Embassy of the Federal Republic of Germany, Embassy of Japan, Royal Netherlands Embassy, Royal Norwegian Embassy, Spanish Embassy, Embassy of Sweden, New Zealand High Commission, and the British Embassy, Helsinki.

I should also like to thank the following: Bengt Grundberg, G.P. Humphreys, Gillian Lindsey, Brian Mairs, Brian Toward, Nicholas Paxton, and my two friends Dione Daffin and Penny White for much hard work typing and for spotting inconsistencies.

Preface

IN 1974 I wrote in the preface to my *Everyman Dictionary of Abbreviations*: "The manufacture of abbreviations remains one of the largest and fastest growing industries in the world today". That is still true in 2002.

The military used to invent more abbreviations than anybody but computers and technology soon caught up. Medicine contributes many, as does sport. The financial world is quite active but in recent years this has accelerated and the publishers and I have decided that a separate dictionary is necessary.

An enormous number of abbreviations, acronyms, contractions, initialisms, and symbols are created each week but most are forgotten by the end of the month. In this dictionary I've attempted to cover the fields of commerce, finance, banking, and accounting, but have also included large international organizations particularly where they have large budgets and influence financial activity. Trade unions and employers' organizations are included. I have not, with a few exceptions, included initials used by big corporations as their corporate names. I've included a few entries that are not abbreviations, although they look like them, such as CREST and ProShare. Currencies may have several entries, the ones used by the international banking community have "international currency symbol" at the end of the entry. Some entries have extended explanatory text. Finally, although the dictionary is international in content, UK and US entries tend to dominate.

I would be grateful to hear from readers who have suggestions for the improvement and extension of the present work. Planting and weeding is an important ongoing activity for dictionary compilers.

JOHN PAXTON
Bruton, Somerset,
ENGLAND
April 2002

A

A	*accepté*. Accepted. (France)
A	accepted
A	*akzeptiert*. Accepted. (Germany)
$A	Australian dollar divided into 100 cents (also currency of Norfolk Island, Nauru, Tuvalu, and Kiribati)
AA	Associate in Accounting
AA	attendance allowance (UK)
AAI	Indicating a very high quality rating for credit
AAA	American Academy of Actuaries
AAA	American Accounting Association. Association that influences the development of generally accepted accounting principles through published research of its professional membership.
AAA	Association of Average Adjusters. Founded in London in 1869.
AAA	Australian Association of Accountants
AAA	Top rating for bonds given by the US rating agencies Standard & Poor's (**S&P**) and Moody's. The range for top-grade (investment-grade) bonds is from AAA (Aaa with Moody's) down to BBB- (Baa3). Lower-grade or junk bonds range from BB+ (Ba1) down to B- (B3). High default risk ratings are graded CCC (Caa) and an issuer who fails to meet scheduled interest or principal payment is graded C (Moody's) and D (Standard & Poor's). The lower the credit rating, the higher the interest the bond has to pay.
AAA-CPA	American Association of Attorney-Certified Public Accountants
AAAI	Associate of the Institute of Administrative Accountants, now known as the Institute of Financial Accountants; *see* **AFA**
AABL	Associated Australian Banks in London
AACB	Associate of the Association of Certified Book-Keepers
AACB	Association of African Central Banks
AACC	American Association of Credit Counsellors
AACCA	Associate of the Association of Certified and Corporate Accountants

11

AACI	Accredited Appraiser Canadian Institute
AACP	Anglo-American Council on Productivity
AACSB	American Assembly of Collegiate Schools of Business. Recognized agency that accredits programmes in accounting and business administration.
AACT	American Association of Commodity Traders
AADFI	Association of African Development Finance Institutions. Established in 1975 to encourage and support funding for economic and social development projects in African countries.
AAFC	Air Accounting and Finance Centre
AAFC	Associate of the Association of Financial Controllers and Administrators
AAFI	Associated Accounting Firms International
AAHA	American Association of Hospital Accountants
AAIA	Associate of the Association of International Accountants
AAIB	Associate of the Australian Institute of Bankers
AAII	American Association of Individual Investors. Chicago-based organization providing educational and networking opportunities and publications for the individual investor.
AAII	Associate of the Australian Insurance Institute
AAL	actuarial accrued liability
AAPA	Association of Authorised Public Accountants, *also* Associate of the Association of Authorised Public Accountants
AAPC	Adjusted average per capita cost. Term relating to adjustments made to average per capita costs to increase the accuracy of an analysis.
AAR	against all risks (insurance)
AARF	Australian Accounting Research Foundation
AARP	annual advance retainer pay
AARS	accrual accounting and reporting system
AAS	advanced accounting system
AASA	Associate of the Australian Society of Accountants
AASC	Australian Accounting Standards Committee
AASE	Australian Associated Stock Exchange
AAT	Association of Accounting Technicians
AATMA	Australian Association of Taxation and Management Accountants

AAUQ	Associate in Accountancy University of Queensland (Australia)
AAUTA	Australian Association of University Teachers of Accounting
aB	*auf Bestellung*. On order. (Germany)
A/B	*Aktiebolaget*. Joint stock company. (Sweden)
ABA	American Bankers Association. Professional association offering programmes, products, and services for the banking community.
ABA	American Bar Association
ABA	Annual Budget Authorization
ABA	Associate in Business Administration
ABA	Australian Bankers' Association
ABAA	Associate of British Association of Accountants and Auditors
ABAJ	*American Bar Association Journal*
ABB	*abbuno*. Discount. (Italy)
ABB	activity-based budgeting
ABBB	Association of Better Business Bureaus
ABCC	Association of British Chambers of Commerce
ABERCOR	Associated Banks of Europe Corporation
ABI	Associate of the Book-keepers Institute
ABI	Association of British Insurers. Trade association formed in 1985 by a merger of the British Insurance Association (**BIA**) with the Life Insurance Association and the Life Offices Association and other bodies. Its objects are to represent members' interests to government and to political and trade bodies in general.
ABIA	Associate of the Bankers' Institute of Australia
ABINZ	Associate of the Bankers' Institute of New Zealand
ABLA	American Business Law Association
ABM	Associate in Business Management
ABN	American Bank Note
ABNCO	American Bank Note Company
ABO	Association of Buying Offices
ABR	Accredited Buyer Representative
ABR	*American Bankruptcy Reports*
ABRM	Accredited Buyer Representative Manager

ABS	asset-backed securities. Bonds or notes backed by loans or accounts receivable originated by banks, credit card companies, or other providers of credit.
ABS	Associate of the Building Societies Institute
ABS	automated bond system. Computerized system used by the New York Stock Exchange (**NYSE**) for recording bids and offers for inactively traded bonds until they are cancelled or executed.
AC	*a compté*. On account. (France)
AC	average cost
A/C	account
A/C	account current
ACA	Accreditation Council for Accountancy
ACA	Associate of the Institute of Chartered Accountants in England and Wales, or Ireland
ACA	Association of Consulting Actuaries
ACAA	Associate of the Australasian Institute of Cost Accountants
ACAS	Advisory, Conciliation and Arbitration Service. UK authority established in 1975 to provide counselling services for industrial relations and employment policy matters, in particular mediation, conciliation, and arbitration in cases of industrial dispute.
ACAS	Associate of the Casualty Actuarial Society
ACAT	automated customer account transfer
ACAUS	Association of Chartered Accountants in the USA. Association of Chartered Accountants from Australia, Canada, England and Wales, Ireland, New Zealand, Scotland, and South Africa who are based in the USA.
ACB	America's Community Bankers
ACB	Arkansas Community Bankers' Association (US)
ACB	Association of Certified Book-keepers (UK)
ACB	Association of Customers' Brokers
ACB of A	Associated Credit Bureaus of America
ACBS	Accrediting Commission of Business Schools
ACBs	Associated Credit Bureaus
ACBSI	Associate of the Chartered Building Societies Institute
ACC	acceptance, bill of exchange
ACC	Accident Compensation Corporation (New Zealand)

ACC	account
ACC	Agricultural Credit Corporation
ACC	annual capital charge
ACCA	Association of Chartered Certified Accountants, *also* Associate of
ACC & AUD	
	accountant and auditor
ACCFA	Agricultural Credit Cooperative Finance Administration
ACCI	Association Canadian Condominium Institute
ACCS	Associate of the Corporation of Secretaries
ACCT	account
ACCT	accountant
ACCT	accounting
ACCY	accountancy
ACEA	Associate of the Institute of Cost and Executive Accountants
ACEd	Associate in Commercial Education
ACEF	Association of Commodity Exchange Firms
ACES	Advanced Computerized Execution System. System run by the National Association of Securities Dealers (**NASD**), which owns and operates the National Association of Securities Dealers Automated Quotation System (**NASDAQ**).
ACFA	Association of Commercial Finance Attorneys
ACH	Automated Clearing House, *now* known as Electronic Payments Network (**EPN**) (US)
ACIA	Associate of the Corporation of Insurance Agents
ACIArb	Associate of the Chartered Institute of Arbitrators
ACIB	Associate of the Chartered Institute of Bankers
ACIB	Associate of the Corporation of Insurance Brokers
ACIBS	Associate of the Chartered Institute of Bankers in Scotland
ACII	Associate of the Chartered Insurance Institute
ACILA	Associate of the Chartered Institute of Loss Adjusters
ACIS	Associate of the Institute of Chartered Secretaries and Administrators
ACMA	Associate of the Chartered Institute of Management Accountants
AcommA	Associate of the Society of Commercial Accountants

ACP   African, Caribbean, and Pacific States. Term given to the developing countries that have an association agreement with the **EU** under Articles 131–136 of the Treaties of Rome. While the original provisions were directed towards the former colonies of the Six, and documented by the 1963 and 1969 Yaoundé Conventions, the enlargement of the Community has brought new members into the agreement, which, since 1975, has fallen under the Lomé Convention. There are now some 70 states linked to the EU under the Fourth Lomé Convention, which was agreed in 1990, and these states are eligible for grants from the **EIB** and **EDF**.

ACPA   Associate of the Institute of Certified Public Accountants (US)

ACPA   Associate of the Institute of Certified Public Accountants in Ireland

ACPAE   Association of Certified Public Accounts Examiners

A/C PAY   accounts payable

ACRS   accelerated cost recovery system

ACS   Association of Caribbean States. The Convention establishing the ACS was signed on 24 July 1994 in Cartagena de Indias, Colombia, with the aim of promoting integration among all the countries of the Caribbean. Members are Antigua and Barbuda, Bahamas, Barbados, Belize, Colombia, Costa Rica, Cuba, Dominica, Dominican Republic, El Salvador, Grenada, Guatemala, Guyana, Haiti, Honduras, Jamaica, Mexico, Nicaragua, Panama, St Kitts and Nevis, St Lucia, St Vincent and the Grenadines, Suriname, Trinidad and Tobago, and Venezuela. The ACS is an organization for consultation, cooperation, and concerted action in the context of economic integration and functional cooperation. Its objectives are enshrined in the Convention and are focused on the following: strengthening of the regional cooperation and integration process, with a view to creating an enhanced economic space in the region; preserving the environmental integrity of the Caribbean Sea which is regarded as the common patrimony of the peoples of the region; and promoting the sustainable development of the Great Caribbean.

ACSA   Associate of the Institute of Chartered Secretaries and Administrators

AcSEC   Accounting Standards Executive Committee. American Institute of Certified Public Accountants Committee whose objective is to determine **AICPA** technical policies regarding financial accounting and reporting standards. AcSEC provides guidance, through Statements of Position, Audit and Accounting Guides, and Practice Bulletins, on practice or industry financial accounting or reporting issues until the Financial Accounting Standards Board or Governmental Accounting Standards Board provides guidance in those areas.

A/CS PAY   accounts payable

A/CS REC   accounts receivable

ACT   advance corporation tax. Corporation tax is a UK tax levied on the assessable profits of companies. Several countries, including the US and the UK, have a lower rate of tax for smaller companies.

ACT   Association of Corporate Treasurers. Established 1979. (UK)

A CTA   *a cuenta*. On account. (Spain)

ACU   Asian Currency Unit

ACUTE   Accountants Computer Users for Technical Exchange

ACWA   Associate of the Institute of Costs and Works Accountants, *now* **ACMA**

AD   accidental damage (insurance)

AD   account day, date on which payment is due by customers, brokers, and jobbers

A & D   accounting and disbursing

ADB   African Development Bank. Established in 1964 to promote economic and social development in the region. Regional members are Algeria, Angola, Benin, Botswana, Burkina Faso, Burundi, Cameroon, Cape Verde, Central African Republic, Chad, Comoros, Congo (Republic of), Congo (Democratic Republic of), Côte d'Ivoire, Djibouti, Egypt, Equatorial Guinea, Eritrea, Ethiopia, Gabon, The Gambia, Ghana, Guinea, Guinea–Bissau, Kenya, Lesotho, Liberia, Libya, Madagascar, Malawi, Mali, Mauritania, Mauritius, Morocco, Mozambique, Namibia, Niger, Nigeria, Rwanda, São Tomé e Príncipe, Senegal, Seychelles, Sierra Leone, Somalia, South Africa (Republic of), Sudan, Swaziland, Tanzania, Togo, Tunisia, Uganda, Zambia, and Zimbabwe. Nonregional members are Argentina, Austria, Belgium, Brazil, Canada, China, Denmark, Finland, France, Germany, India, Italy, Japan, Korea (Republic of), Kuwait, Netherlands, Norway, Portugal, Saudi Arabia, Spain, Sweden, Switzerland, UK, and USA.

ADB   Asian Development Bank. Multilateral development financial institution established in 1966 by 32 governments mainly in

Asia but including those of the USA, the UK, and Switzerland. The bank provides financial aid to the developing countries in the Pacific and Asian regions. The bank give special attention to the needs of smaller or less developed countries, giving priority to regional, sub-regional, and national projects which contribute to the economic growth of the region and promote regional cooperation. Loans from ordinary capital resources on non-concessional terms account for about 80 per cent of cumulative lending. Loans from the bank's principal special fund, the Asian Development Fund, are made on highly concessional terms almost exclusively to the poorest borrowing countries.

ADC   advanced developing country

ADC   Agricultural Development Corporation (Jamaica)

ADC   analog-digital converter

ADC   automatic digital calculator

ADEF   Agence d'evaluation financière. French rating agency.

ADF   approved deposit fund (Australia)

ADJ   adjustment

ADP   Automatic Data Processing. Data processing achieved by computer.

ADR   American depository receipt. Investment certificate for shares of foreign-based corporation held in a US bank. Shareholders are entitled to dividends and capital gains. These securities are traded on US stock exchanges.

ADR   asset depreciation range

ADR   automatic dividend reinvestment. Investment term for a programme in which dividends of a company are directly reinvested rather than paid out as dividend.

ADS   American depository share. Most common means by which US investors hold shares in non-US companies. It represents shares in the non-US company and carries similar rights to those conferred by ordinary shares, including the right to receive any dividend paid by the company. *Also* known as American depository receipt (ADR).

ADS   annual debt service. Term for total annual amount paid by an investor in connection with a long-term loan.

ADSN   Accounting and Disbursing Station Number

ADST   approved deferred share trust

AD VAL   *ad valorem*. According to value.

ADX	Average Directional Movement. Index that measures the strength of a prevailing trend.
AEC	additional extended coverage (insurance)
AED	United Arab Emirates, dirham (international currency symbol)
AEI	average earnings index
AEIBC	American Express International Banking Corporation
AEIDC	American Express International Development Company
AEL	audit error list
AEP	accrued expenditure paid
AER	annual equivalent rate. Usually specifies the interest paid from current, deposit, or savings accounts. This new term replaces Compound Annual Rate **CAR**.
AES	annual expectation of sales
AESOP	all-employee share ownership plan
AEU	accrued expenditure unpaid
AEX	Amsterdam Exchanges. Equity and derivatives market formed in Amsterdam through the merger in 1997 of the Amsterdam Stock Exchange and the European Options Exchange.
AF	advanced freight
Af	afghani divided into 100 puls (Afghanistan currency)
AFA	Accounting Firms Associated, Inc.
AFA	Afghanistan, afghani (international currency symbol)
AFA	American Finance Association, founded 1939
AFA	Associate of the Faculty of Actuaries in Scotland
AFA	Associate of the Faculty of Auditors
AFA	Associate of the Institute of Financial Accountants
AFAIM	Associate Fellow of the Australian Institute of Management
AFBD	Association of Futures Brokers and Dealers
AfDB	African Development Bank, *see* **ADB**
AFE	Aims for Freedom and Enterprise, founded in 1942 as Aims for Industry, a pressure group to defend and promote capitalism
AFESD	Arab Fund for Economic and Social Development. Fund, established in 1968 but became operational in 1974. Aims to assist member countries to eliminate development constraints, increase capacity and achieve higher rates of

19

growth; and to foster economic integration and cooperation. Members are Algeria, Bahrain, Djibouti, Egypt, Jordan, Kuwait, Lebanon, Libya, Mauritania, Morocco, Oman, Palestine, Qatar, Saudi Arabia, Syria, Tunisia, United Arab Emirates, and Republic of Yemen. Iraq, Somalia, and Sudan were suspended in 1993.

AFFC Air Force Finance Centre

AFI Associate of the Faculty of Insurance

AFIA American Foreign Insurance Association

AFIA Associate of the Federal Institute of Accountants (Australia)

AFIIM Associate Fellow of the Institution of Industrial Managers

AFL-CIO American Federation of Labor and Congress of Industrial Organizations

AFPC Advanced Financial Planning Certificate

AFREXIMBANK
African Export-Import Bank. Established in 1978 under the auspices of the African Development Bank to facilitate, promote, and expand intra-African and extra-African trade.

AFSA American Financial Services Association

AFSBO American Federation of Small Business Organizations

AFT automatic fund transfer

AFTR *American Federal Tax Reports*

AG accountant-general

AG *Aktiengesellschaft*. German public limited company.

AGA American Gold Association

AGA Association of Government Accountants. US organization of **CPA**s and others involved in governmental accounting and auditing at all levels.

AGI adjusted gross income (in US income tax returns)

AGM annual general meeting. Yearly meeting of shareholders which joint-stock companies are required by law to convene, in order to allow shareholders to discuss their company's annual report and accounts, elect directors, and agree the dividend payouts suggested by directors. In USA known as annual meeting or annual stockholders' meeting.

A & H accident and health (insurance)

A & I accident and indemnity (insurance)

AIA American Insurance Association

AIA Associate of the Institute of Actuaries

AIA	Association of International Accountants
AIAB	Associate, International Association of Book-keepers
AIAC	Associate of the Institute of Company Accountants
AIANZ	Associate of the Incorporated Institute of Accountants, New Zealand
AIB	American Institute of Banking
AIB	Anti-Inflation Board
AIB	Associate of the Institute of Bankers
AIBA	American Industrial Bankers Association
AIBD	Association of International Bond Dealers, *now* International Securities Market Association (**ISMA**)
AIBScot	Associate of the Institute of Bankers in Scotland
AIC	Arab Investment Company
AICA	Associate Member of the Commonwealth Institute of Accountants
AICA	Associate of the Institute of Company Accountants
AICB	Associate of the Institute of Certified Book-Keepers
AICM (Cert)	
	Associate Member of the Institute of Credit Management, requires completion of certificate qualification
AICPA	American Institute of Certified Public Accountants, formed in 1887
AICS	Associate of the Institute of Chartered Shipbrokers
AID	Agency for International Development. An organization providing and supporting funding and education from the USA to emerging nations.
AIDF	African Industrial Development Fund
AIEDP	Asian Institute for Economic Development and Planning
AIFA	Association of Independent Financial Advisers (UK)
AIIA	Associate of the Insurance Institute of America
AIM	Alternative Investment Market. Alternative Investment Market was established in the UK in 1995 and was designed for shares of emerging or small companies that could not fulfil all the requirements of the London Stock Exchange for a full quotation. It replaced the Unlisted Securities Market (**USM**). The AIM allows companies to raise capital, secure a listing, and offer shares for trading, without the strict listing requirement of the main exchange. Companies provide

information including evidence of establishment as a public company, with freely transferable shares, the publication of annual and interim accounts, and the observance by the director of a model code. In addition, AIM companies must appoint a nominated adviser and a nominated broker; the first of these advises and informs the directors of their responsibilities under AIM rules, the second promotes trading in the shares of the firm.

AIM　　Amsterdam Interprofessional Market. Method, initiated on the Amsterdam Stock Exchange in 1986, of transacting business at negotiated commission between banks and commission houses, and institutional investors, thus avoiding services of brokers, or hoekmen.

AIM　　Australian Institute of Management

AIMC　　Associate of the Institute of Management Consultancy

AIMgt　　Associate of the Institute of Management

AIMR　　Association for Investment Management and Research (US)

AInstAM　　Associate of the Institute of Administrative Management

AInstSMM　　Associate of the Institute of Sales and Marketing Management

AIS　　Accounting Information System

AISA　　Associate of the Incorporated Secretaries Association

AISMA　　Association of Independent Specialist Medical Accountants (UK)

AIT　　Association of HM Inspectors of Taxes

AIT　　Association of Investment Trusts

AITC　　Association of Investment Trust Companies. Industry trade body of UK investment trusts, established in 1932.

AJE　　adjusting journal entry

AKT　　*Aktiebolagetg*. Swedish joint stock company.

AKTGES　　*Aktiengesellschaft*. Joint stock company or corporation in Germany.

AKTIES　　*Aktieselkab*. Swedish joint stock company.

AL　　allotment letter

ALACHA　　Alabama Automated Clearing House Association (US)

ALC　　accelerated loan commitment. Term for voluntary acceleration of payments by a borrower, generally to decrease interest payments over the life of the loan.

ALC　　Accredited Land Consultant. ALCs are the recognized experts in land brokerage transactions of five specialized types: (i) farms and ranches; (ii) undeveloped tracts of land; (iii) transitional and development land; (iv) subdivision and wholesaling of lots; and (v) site selection and assemblage of land parcels.

ALE(S) additional living expense(s)

ALFI Luxembourg Investment Funds Association

ALGFO Association of Local Government Finance Officers

ALIA (dip) Associate, Life Insurance Association (Diploma)

ALL Albania, lek (international currency symbol)

ALM Association of Lloyd's Members. Non-official association of external members of Lloyd's, created to inform and advise members on Lloyd's issues, and to represent the views of members.

ALM asset-liability management

ALR *American Law Reports*

ALT alternative trading system

AMA American Management Association

AMAS Automatic Message Accounting System

AMBAC American Municipal Bond Assurance Corporation. US government oversight organization involved with municipal bond issues.

AM BANKR REPS
American Bankruptcy Reports

AMC Agricultural Mortgage Corporation

AMC Association of Management Consultants

AmCham-EU
EU Committee of the American Chamber of Commerce

AMCIA Associate Member of the Association of Cost and Industrial Accountants

AMCIB Associate Member of the Corporation of Insurance Brokers

AMCOM American Stock Exchange Communications

AMCT Associate Member of the Association of Corporate Treasurers

AMD Armenia, dram (international currency symbol)

AMEX American Express

AMEX American Stock Exchange. New York Stock Exchange listing smaller and less mature companies than those listed on

23

the larger New York Stock Exchange (**NYSE**). Also known as the Little Board and the Curb Exchange.

AMEXCO   American Express Company

AMF   Arab Monetary Fund. Established in 1976 the Fund aims to assist member countries in eliminating payments and trade restrictions, in achieving exchange rate stability, in developing capital markets and in correcting payments imbalances through the extension of short- and medium-term loans; to coordinate monetary policies of member countries; and to liberalize and promote trade and payments, as well as to encourage capital flows among member countries. Members include Algeria, Bahrain, Comoros, Djibouti, Egypt, Iraq, Jordan, Kuwait, Lebanon, Libya, Mauritania, Morocco, Oman, Palestine, Qatar, Saudi Arabia, Somalia, Sudan, Syria, Tunisia, United Arab Emirates, and the Republic of Yemen.

AMGOLD   Anglo-American Gold Investment Trust

AMIA   Affiliate Member of the Association of International Accountants

AMIEX   Associate Member of the Institute of Export

AMIS   Alternative Mortgage Instruments Study

AMMINET   Automated Mortgage Management Information Network

AMO   Accredited Management Organization

AMOS   American Stock Exchange Switching System

AMPS   auction market preferred stock. Type of adjustable-rate preferred stock in which the dividend is determined every seven weeks in an auction process whereby the price is gradually lowered until it meets a responsive bid from a corporate bidder.

AMS   Agricultural Marketing Service. Service of the US government which assures purchasers of US goods that they satisfy quality standards and contractual commitments.

AMT   alternative minimum tax

AMUE   Association for the Monetary Union of Europe

AMVI   **AMEX** Market Value Index. One of two major market indexes compiled by the American Stock Exchange.

ANB & TC   American National Bank and Trust Company

ANG   Netherlands Antilles, guilder, gulden, or florin (**Na f**) (international currency symbol)

ANI   American Nuclear Insurers

ANN   annuity

ANOVA   analysis of variance

ANRPC   Association of Natural Rubber Producing Countries. Inter-governmental organization, formed 1970, comprising India, Indonesia, Malaysia, Papua New Guinea, Singapore, Sri Lanka, and Thailand. Its aim is to bring about coordination in production and marketing, to promote technical co-operation among member countries, and to achieve fair and stable prices.

ANTO   Accountancy National Trading Organization (UK), *now* part of Accountancy Occupational Standards Group

ANTR   apparent net transfer rate

ANZ   Australia and New Zealand Banking Group

AO   account of

AO   accountant officer

AO   *Ahonim Ortalik*. Turkish joint stock company.

AOAD   Arab Organization for Agricultural Development. The AOAD commenced operations in 1972. Its aims are to develop natural and human resources in the agricultural sector and improve the means and methods of exploiting these resources on scientific bases; to increase agricultural productive efficiency and achieve agricultural integration between the Arab states and countries; to increase agricultural production with a view to achieving a higher degree of self-sufficiency; to facilitate the exchange of agricultural products between the Arab states and countries; to enhance the establishment of agricultural ventures and industries; and to increase the standards of living of the labour force engaged in the agricultural sector. Members are Algeria, Bahrain, Djibouti, Egypt, Iraq, Jordan, Kuwait, Lebanon, Libya, Mauritania, Morocco, Oman, Palestine, Qatar, Saudi Arabia, Somalia, Sudan, Syria, Tunisia, United Arab Emirates, and Republic of Yemen.

AOB   annual operating budget

AOK   readjusted kwanza (Angolan currency)

AOM   Australian Options Market. Sydney-based options market.

AON   Angola, new kwanza (international currency symbol)

AOS   automated office system

AOS   automated order system

AP   additional premium (insurance)

APA   additional personal allowance (taxation)

APACS   Association for Payment Clearing Services. Umbrella organization for payment clearings in the UK. It operates through three clearing companies: (i) Bankers' Automated Clearing System (**BACS**) is the UK's clearing house for bulk clearing of electronic debits and credits (e.g. direct debits and salary credits); (ii) the Cheque and Credit Clearing Company Ltd operates bulk clearing systems for inter-bank cheques and paper credit items in Great Britain; (iii) Clearing House Automated Payments Systems (**CHAPS**) provides same-day clearing for high-value electronic funds transfers through the UK in sterling and internationally in euros. Membership of APACS and the clearing companies is open to any appropriately regulated financial institution providing payment services and meeting the relevant membership criteria. Membership comprises the major banks and building societies.

APB   Accounting Principles Board. Former US standards-setting body for accounting principles operating from 1962–73. Succeeded by Financial Accounting Standards Board (**FASB**).

APB   Auditing Practices Board (*formerly* Auditing Practices Committee). Responsible for developing and issuing standards for auditors in the UK and Republic of Ireland.

APC   Auditing Practices Committee, *now* Auditing Practices Board

APC   average propensity to consume. The proportion of a given level of national income which is spent on consumption.

APCIMS   Association of Private Client Investment Managers and Stockbrokers. The official body of fund managers and stockbrokers in the UK that specialize in providing investment services for private clients.

APE   annual premium equivalent. Regular premium plus 10 per cent of one-off payments.

APEC   Asia-Pacific Economic Cooperation Forum. Grouping, founded 1989, of the governments of 21 countries bordering the Pacific, comprising those in the Far East, Australasia, and the Americas, for the purpose of the liberalization of trade and investment, and to promote economic and technical cooperation between its members. Members are Australia, Brunei, Canada, Chile, China, Hong Kong, Indonesia, Japan, Korea (Republic of), Malaysia, Mexico, New Zealand, Papua New Guinea, Peru, Philippines, Russia, Singapore, Taiwan, Thailand, USA, and Vietnam.

APFA   Asia Pacific Finance Association

APMI   Associate of the Pensions Management Institute

APR   annual purchase rate (in hire purchase schemes)

APR	annualized percentage rate. Annualized percentage rate of interest charged on a loan. The APR rate will depend on the total charge for credit applied by the lender and will be influenced by such factors as the general level of interest rates, and the nature and duration of the loan. Until the Truth in Lending Act in the USA and the Consumer Credit Act in the UK the percentage was generally shown as the rate per month – a rate smaller than the rate per annum.
APT	arbitrage pricing theory
APT	Automated Pit Trading, the **LIFFE** screen-based trading system
APV	adjusted present value
AQL	acceptable quality level. Highest proportion of rejects from a sample of raw materials, work in progress, or finished goods that will be tolerated by a business.
ARA	Accounting Research Association
ARA	Accredited Rural Appraiser
ARBs	Arbitrageurs. Executives who buy shares in companies subject to takeover bids.
ARDC	Agricultural Refinance and Development Corporation
ARIA	Accounting Researchers International Association
ARICS	Professional Associate of the Royal Institution of Chartered Surveyors
ARIEL	Automated Real-time Investments Exchange Limited (former computerized share-dealing system)
ARLA	Association of Retail Letting Agents
ARM	Accredited Resident Manager
ARM	adjustable rate mortgage. Mortgage loan, in the USA, in which the rate of interest is adjusted in line with market interest rates at predetermined intervals.
ARO	asset retirement obligation
ARP	Argentina, peso (international currency symbol)
ARPS	adjustable rate preferred stock. A form of preference shares in the USA, for which dividends are linked to the rates of interest on treasury bills. ARPs are convertible into common stocks at a fixed price at a specified date or dates.
ARR	accounting rate of return. Method of valuing shares in a company where the estimated future profits are divided by the rate of return required by the investors.
ARR	average rate of return

ARS	Annual Report to Shareholders
ARSC	Accounting and Review Services Committee. Committee under the American Institute of **CPA**s.
ART	Alternative Risk Transfer
ARTIS	Austrian Real-Time Interbank Settlement
ARVA	Associate of the Rating and Valuation Association
A & S	accident and sickness (insurance)
AS	*Anonim Sirket*. Turkish joint stock company.
A/S	after sight
A/S	*Aksjeselskap*. Norwegian joint stock company.
A/S	*Aktieselkab*. Danish joint stock company.
ASA	Accredited Senior Appraiser
ASA	Advertising Standards Authority. Body that regulates the advertising industry in the UK to ensure that advertisements provide a fair, honest, and unambiguous representation of the products they promote.
ASA	Associate of the Society of Actuaries in the USA
ASA	Australian Society of Accountants
ASAA	Associate of the Society of Incorporated Accountants and Auditors, *now* amalgamated with **ACA**
ASB	Accounting Standards Board. The Accounting Standards Board sets accounting standards for the UK. It issues Financial Reporting Standards (**FRS**) and in 1990 replaced the Accounting Standards Committee (**ASC**) which issued Statements of Standard Accounting Practice (**SSAP**).
ASB	Auditing Standards Board. Board authorized by the American Institute of Certified Public Accountants (**AICPA**) to promulgate auditing and attest standards, procedures, and implementation guidance for AICPA members performing such services.
ASC	Accounting Standards Committee (from 1990, Accounting Standards Board, **ASB**)
ASC	Australian Securities Commission. Supervisory body for securities transactions in Australia.
ASCA	Associate of the Institute of Company Accountants. *Formerly* Associate of the Society of Company and Commercial accountants, but earlier designating letters retained.
ASCIE	American Standard Code and Information Exchange
ASDA	American Safe Deposit Association

ASE   American Stock Exchange, more frequently known as **AMEX**

ASE   Amsterdam Stock Exchange

ASE   Athens Stock Exchange

ASEAN   Association of South East Asian Nations. ASEAN is a regional intergovernmental organization formed by the governments of Indonesia, Malaysia, the Philippines, Singapore, and Thailand through the Bangkok Declaration which was signed by the foreign ministers on 8 August 1967. Brunei joined in 1984, Vietnam in 1995, Laos and Myanmar in 1997, and Cambodia in 1999. Papua New Guinea also has observer status. The main objectives are to accelerate economic growth, social progress, and cultural development; to promote active collaboration and mutual assistance in matters of common interest; to ensure the political and economic stability of the South East Asian region; and to maintain close cooperation with existing international and regional organizations with similar aims.

ASFA   Associate of the Society of Financial Advisers

A Shares   shares in a company that give holders no voting rights

ASI   Asian Statistical Institute

ASIP   Associate Member of the UK Society of Investment Professionals

AS & LB   American Savings and Loan Bank

ASOBAT   *A Statement of Basic Accounting Theory*. Published by the American Accounting Association.

ASP   *accepté sous protêt*. Accepted under protest.

ASP   American selling price

ASPF   Association of Superannuation and Pension Funds

ASSOBANCA
               Associazione Bancaria Italiana. Italian Bankers' Association.

AST   automated screen trading. Electronic dealing system in which orders to buy or sell are entered, matched, and carried out on a computer system and at prices shown in video terminals. Such a system eliminates telephone dealing and paperwork and therefore liaising with trading floors and back offices.

ASWA   American Society of Women Accountants

ASX   Australian Stock Exchange. There were formerly six stock exchange trading floors in Australia: in Adelaide, Brisbane, Hobart, Melbourne, Perth, and Sydney. The formation of the national stock exchange in April 1987 amalgamated the six state exchanges, loosely federated in the Australian Associated Stock Exchange (**AASE**), into one body.

ATA	American Taxation Association
ATA	American Taxpayers' Association
ATBI	Allied Trades of the Banking Industry
ATF	accounting tabulating form
ATII	Associate of the Chartered Institute of Taxation; *formerly* Associate of the Taxation Institution Incorporated
ATL	actual total loss (insurance)
ATM	automated teller machine. Computerized machine used by banks for paying or withdrawing money, statement inquiries, and transfers. Operated by magnetic stripe "swipe" cards and personal identification numbers (**PIN**s).
ATP	aid trade provision
ATPC	Association of Tin Producing Countries. Association of tin-mining countries (Australia, Bolivia, Indonesia, Malaysia, Nigeria, Thailand, and Democratic Republic of Congo) formed in 1985.
ATRA	American Tort Reform Association. Coalition of associations, nonprofit organizations, consumer advocates, businesses, and professionals whose purpose is to restore fairness, balance, and predictability to the nation's civil justice system.
ATRM	American Tax Reduction Movement
ATRSO	accepts transfer as offered
ATS	alternative trading system
ATS	automated trade system. An electronic system for trading on the New Zealand Futures and Options Exchange.
ATS	Austria, schilling (*former* currency, *now* euro), international currency symbol
ATT	Member of the Association of Taxation Technicians
ATX Index	Main Vienna Stock Exchange share index
AU	African Union, *formerly* Organization of African Unity
AUD	audit
AUD	auditor
AUD	Australia, dollar (international currency symbol)
AUDDIS	automated direct debit instruction service
AUD DISB	auditor disbursements
AUD.GEN	auditor-general

AUNTIE automatic unit for national taxation and insurance

AUTA Association of University Teachers of Accounting

AUTIF Association of Unit Trusts and Investment Funds. Founded in the UK in 1959 as the Association of Unit Trust Managers, AUTIF is a trade association for unit trust managers with a membership that includes banks, building societies, insurance companies, stockbrokers, and investment management houses.

AV *ad valorem*. According to value.

AVC additional voluntary contribution. Additional cost paid by an individual into a company pension scheme to improve the benefits he/she will receive on retirement.

AWB Agricultural Wages Board

AWF Aruba, florin (international currency symbol)

AWSCPA American Women's Society of Certified Public Accountants

AZM Azerbaijan, manat (international currency symbol)

B

B	Thai baht (currency)
B	Balboa (Panamanian currency)
B	Bolivar divided into 100 centimos (Venezuelan currency)
B	Boliviano divided into 100 centavos (Bolivian currency)
B2B	business to business
B$	Bahamian dollar divided into 100 cents (currency)
B$	Brunei dollar divided into 100 cents (currency)
BA	balancing allowance
BA	bank/banker's acceptance
BA	benefit agency. Executive agency of the UK Department of Social Security
BA	Bureau of Accounts
BAA	British Accounting Association. Association of accounting academics
BAA&A	British Association of Accountants and Auditors
BAAEC	Board of Accreditation of Accountancy Education Courses
BAC	Business Archives Council
BACB	British Association of Communicators in Business
B ACC	Bachelor of Accountancy
BACH	Base for the Accountants of Companies Harmonized. Database of statistical data on company accounts. (EU)
BACIE	British Association for Commercial and Industrial Education
BACS	Bankers' Automated Clearing Service
BADEA	Banque arabe pour le développement économique en Afrique. Arab Bank for Economic Development in Africa.
BA & F	budget, accounting and finance
BAG	Bank Action Group
BAHA	British Association of Hospitality Accountants
BAI	Bank Administration Institute
BAI	Bank of America International
BAK	Bosnia-Hercegovina, convertible marka (international currency symbol)

BAKred Bundesaufsichtsamt für das Kreditwesen. Federal German Supervisory Office for Credit. It is responsible for banking business and the regulation of investment activity by funds such as unit trusts.

BAL balance

BALPA balance of payments

BAM Bosnia-Hercegovina marka (currency)

BAN bond anticipation note. Short-term borrowing that serves as an interim source of funds for a project that is eventually to be financed by the sale of bonds. (US)

BANCO El Banco. World Bank for Reconstruction and Development. (Spain)

BANKCAL Bank of California

BANKERS Bankers Publishing (Boston)

BANKERS Bankers Trust (New York)

BANKPAC Bankers Political Action Committee

BANKS CLGS
bank clearings

BANTSA Bank of American National Trust and Savings Association

BAO bankruptcy annulment order

BAP Beta Alpha Psi. US premier professional accounting and business information fraternity which recognizes academic excellence and complements members' formal education by providing for interaction among students, faculty, and professionals.

BAP *billets à payer*. Bills payable. (France)

BAQ basic allowance for quarters

BAR *billets à recevoir*. Bills receivable. (France)

BARIC Baric Computing Services, owned by ICO and Barclays Bank

BARONS Business-Accounts Reporting Operating Network System

BASE Bank-Americard Service Exchange

BAU business as usual

BAWe Bundesaufsichtsamt für den Wertpapierhandel. German Federal Supervisory Office for Securities Trading.

BB Banco do Brasil. Bank of Brazil.

BB bank book

BB bank burglar(y)

BB   *Blue Book*. UK official annual publication published by the Office for National Statistics that gives details of National Income.

BB   Bureau of the Budget

BBA   British Bankers' Association

BBB   banker's blanket bond

BBB   Better Business Bureau. Any of a group of local organizations in the USA, supported by businessmen, functioning to receive and investigate customer complaints about area businesses and make their findings available to the general public.

BBC   Bank of British Columbia

BBD   Barbados, dollar (international currency symbol)

BB (DCO) Barclays Bank (Dominion, Colonial, and Overseas), *now* Barclays International

BBL   Bangkok Bank Limited

BBL   Barclays Bank Limited

bbls   barrels

BBQC   British Board of Quality Control

BBSU   big bond service undertaking

BC   bad check or bogus cheque. Banking term for a cheque uncollectable because either the account has insufficient funds or the cheque itself is fraudulent.

BC   Banco Central. Central Bank of Spain.

BC   bankruptcy court

B/C   bills for collection

B of C   Bank of Canada

BCBS   Basel Committee on Banking Supervision. A commission established by the **G10** central banks.

BCC   British Chambers of Commerce

BCC   British Copyright Council

BCCI   Bank of Credit and Commerce International, *now* liquidated

BCCR   Banco Central de Costa Rica

BCE   Banco Central Europeo (Spain), Banque centrale européenne (France), An Banc Ceannais Eorpach (Ireland), Banca centrale europea (Italy), Banco Central Europeu (Portugal). European Central Bank (**ECB**).

BCE   Board of Customs and Excise

BCEAO Banque central des états de l'Afrique de l'Ouest. Central Bank of West African States. Established in 1962, BCEAO is the common central bank of the member states (Benin, Burkina Faso, Côte d'Ivoire, Guinea–Bissau, Mali, Niger, Senegal, and Togo), which form the West African Monetary Union (**WAMU**). It has the sole right of currency issues throughout the Union territory and is responsible for the pooling of the Union's foreign exchange reserve; the management of the monetary policy of the member states; the keeping of the accounts of the member states treasury; and the definition of the banking law applicable to banks and financial establishments.

BCECC British and Central-European Chamber of Commerce

BCF Bureau of Commercial Fisheries

BCG matrix
Boston Consultancy Group matrix

BCN Banque Canadienne Nationale. Canadian National Bank.

BCP Budget Change Proposal. General business and accounting document for submitting a request for a revision to an existing budget or business plan.

BCPIT British Council for the Promotion of International Trade

BCTA British Canadian Trade Association

BD Bahrain dinar divided into 1000 fils (currency)

BD bank draft. Banking term for conventional paper check/cheque.

BD bond

B/D bank/banker's draft

B/D barrels (of oil) per day

B/D bills discounted

B/D brought down

BD$ Bermuda dollar

BD$ Barbados dollar

B7D buyer has seven days to pay

BDEF Banco de Fomento. Development Bank of Puerto Rico.

BDEF Banque de France. Bank of France.

BDEM Banque de Mexico. Bank of Mexico.

BDEP Banque de Paris. Bank of Paris.

BDI Bundesverband der deutschen Industrie. Federal Association of German Industry.

BDMA   British Direct Marketing Association

BDMAA   British Direct Mail Advertising Association

BD RTS   bond rights

BDT   Bangladesh, taka (international currency symbol)

BDV   Budget Day Value. Value of an asset on 6 April 1965; used in capital gains tax (**CGT**) calculations, as this was the day on which the tax was introduced. (UK)

BDZ   Borsen-Data Zentrale. Computerized stock exchange. (Germany)

BE   Bachelor of Economics

BE   bill of exchange. General business term for documentation involved in exchange (as opposed to purchase or sale) of goods or services.

B/E   bill of entry

B/E   break-even point. General business term for number of units at which total direct and indirect costs connected with a programme, product or service, are equal to revenue from sales of the same number of units, and beyond which sales begin to produce a profit.

B of E   Bank of England. Established in 1694 as the result of a proposal by Scottish merchant William Paterson, the Bank of England is one of the oldest central banks. However its original purposes and functions were very different from its present ones. It started as a commercial bank with private shareholders and developed a large private banking business. It was not until 1946 that it was brought into state ownership but for many years before that the Bank had seen itself, and behaved, as a public institution carrying out public functions. These functions included, from the very start, acting as the government's bank and arranging its borrowing. The Bank has also always had the right to issue bank notes in England and Wales, and acquired the monopoly after the Bank Charter Act of 1844. The same Act accelerated the Bank's withdrawal from commercial banking to concentrate on its role as banker to other banks and to government. This increased its influence over monetary conditions. The Bank also took on a degree of responsibility for maintaining orderly money and capital markets in London and it watched over the soundness of the banks. Affectionately known as "The Old Lady of Threadneedle Street".

BEAC   Banque des états de l'Afrique centrale (Bank of Central African States). BEAC was established in 1973 when a new Convention of Monetary Co-operation with France was signed. The five original members, Cameroon, Central African Republic, Chad, Republic of Congo, and Gabon, were joined by Equatorial Guinea in 1985. Under its Convention and statutes, the BEAC is declared a "Multinational African institution in the management and control of which France participates in return for the guarantee she provides for its currency".

BEACON   Boston Exchange Automated Communication Order-Routing Network. System that permits automatic execution of trades based on the consolidated markets at any of the US securities exchanges.

B EC   Bachelor of Economics

BEC   broad economic categories

BEC   Bureau of Employees' Compensation (US)

B ECON   Bachelor of Economics

B EconPA   Bachelor of Economics in Public Administration

BEF   Belgium, franc (*former* currency, *now* euro), international currency symbol

BEG   Bank Europäischer Genossenschaftsbanken. European Cooperative Bank.

BEHA   British Export Houses Association

BEI   Banque européene d'investissement. European Investments Bank.

BELFOX   Belgian Futures and Options Exchange. Established in 1991 in Brussels and trades in Belgian government bond futures and stock index options.

BEMAC   British Exports Marketing Advisory Committee

BENELUX   Customs union formed by *Bel*gium, the *N*etherlands, and *Lux*embourg in 1948; it became an economic union in 1960

BEPI   budget estimates presentation instructions

BES   Business Expansion Scheme. Former UK scheme aiming to encourage individuals to subscribe and hold on to shares in a small unlisted UK company raising funds to expand. It replaced Business Start-up Scheme (**BSS**) in 1983. Funds up to a specified limit invested in eligible BES companies were fully deductible for tax purposes. The scheme ended in 1994, and was replaced by the Enterprise Investment Scheme (**EIS**).

BESS   Bank of England Statistical Summary

Best   *Bestellung*. Order. (Germany)

BEUC   Bureau européen des unions de consommateurs. European Consumers Organization.

BEXEC   budget execution

BEZ   *bezahlt.* Paid. (Germany)

BF   bankruptcy fee

BF   bring/brought forward

BFA   Bureau of Financial Assistance

BFBPW   British Federation of Business and Professional Women

BFC   Budget and Forecast Calendarization. Accounting and general business term for allocating an annual budget across smaller time periods.

BFCA   British Federation of Commodity Associations

BFE   Baltic Futures Exchange

BFG   Bank für Gemeinwirtschaft. Bank for Municipal Management. (Germany)

BFORM   budget formulation

BFr   Belgian franc, *former* currency, *now* euro

BFR   Belgische frank (Dutch for Belgian franc), *former* currency, *now* euro

BFS   Basic Financial Statements

BGB   Bürgerliches Gesetzbuch. Code of Civil Law. (Germany)

BGC   bank giro credit

BGFO   Bureau of Government Financial Operations

BGL   Bulgaria, lev (international currency symbol)

BGT   bought

BH   Thai baht (currency)

BHD   Bahrain, dinar (international currency symbol)

BHF   Berliner Handels und Frankfurter. German bank.

BI   Banca d'Italia. Bank of Italy.

B & I   bankruptcy and insolvency

BIA   *see* Association of British Insurers (**ABI**)

BIA   business impact assessment

BIBA   *now* **BIIBA**

BIC   Bank Investment Contract. Bank-guaranteed interest on a portfolio providing a specified yield over a specified period of time.

BIC	British Importers Confederation
BIC	Business and Innovation Centres (EU)
BIC	Business in the Community
BICC	Berne International Copyright Convention
BID	Banco Interamericano de Desarrollo. Interamerican Development Bank.
BIDS	British Institute of Dealers in Securities. Trade association of dealers in over-the-counter securities. Now defunct.
BIF	Bank Insurance Fund. A unit of the **FDIC** that provides deposit insurance for banks.
BIF	Burundi, franc (international currency symbol)
BIFFEX	Baltic International Freight Futures Market, *formerly* Baltic International Freight Futures Exchange
BIFN	Banque Internationale pour le Financement de l'Énergie Nucléaire. International Bank for the Financing of Nuclear Energy.
BIFU	Banking, Insurance and Finance Union
BIIBA	British Insurance and Investment Brokers Association. Established in 1977 to represent registered insurance brokers and investment intermediaries.
BIM	British Institute of Management
BIMBO	Buy-in management buy-out
BIMP	Banque Industrielle et Mobilière Privée (France)
BIN	Bank Identification Number. US banking term for number unique to each institution used for automated processing efficiencies.
BIPAR	Bureau Internationale des Producteurs d'Assurance et de Réassurance. International Federation of Insurance Intermediaries.
BIPEL	Banca d'Italia Regolamento Lordo (Italy)
BIPM	Bureau Internationale des Poids et Mésures. International Bureau of Weights and Measures.
BIPS	basis point, *also* **BPS**
BIR	Board of Inland Revenue
BIRF	Banco Internacional de Reconstrucción y Fomento. International Bank for Reconstruction and Development.
BIS	Bachelor in Information Services

BIS   Bank for International Settlements. Established in 1930 with the original aim of settling the question of German World War I reparations, the BIS is the central banks' bank. It aims to promote cooperation between central banks, to provide facilities for international financial operations, and act as agent or trustee in international financial settlements. The 17-member board of directors consists of the governors of the central banks of the following member countries: Belgium, Canada, France, Germany, Italy, Japan, the Netherlands, Sweden, Switzerland, the UK, and the USA. The chairman of the Board acts as president.

BIV   Banco Industrial de Venezuela. Industrial Bank of Venezuela.

BIZ   Bank für Internationalen Zahlungsausgleich. Bank for International Settlements. (Germany)

BK   bank

BKG   banking

BKG   bookkeeping

BKPG   bookkeeping

BKPR   bookkeeper

BKPT   bankrupt

BL   bank larceny

B/L   bill of lading

B & L   building and loan

B & L   business and loan

BLC   balance

BLEU   Belgo-Luxembourg Economic Union. Customs union between Belgium and Luxembourg, established in 1921 and expanded with the creation of **BENELUX**. BLEU resulted in the financial statistics of Belgium and Luxembourg being jointly documented.

BLOX   block order exposure system. Offers to buy or sell large blocks of shares carried in the Teletext Output of Price Information by Computer (**TOPIC**).

BLS   Bureau of Labor Statistics. US government agency that compiles and disseminates national statistics on labour and employment.

BL & SA   Bank of London and South America

BM   Banca Mondiale. World Bank. (Italy)

BM   Banco de Mexico. Bank of Mexico.

BM	Banco Mundial. World Bank. (Portugal, Spain)
BM	Banque du Monde. World Bank. (France)
BM	Bureau of the Mint
B of M	Bank of Montreal
BMA	Bahrain Monetary Agency
BMA	Bond Markets Association
BMA	British Manufacturers' Association
BMD	Bermuda, dollar (international currency symbol)
BM & F	Bolsa de Mercadorias e Futuros. São Paulo, Brazil, Commodities and Futures Exchange, founded 1986. The BM & F is the major commodities and futures exchange of Brazil.
BMRB	British Market Research Bureau
BN	banknote
bn	billion. In the US billion has always been one thousand million, but originally in the UK it meant one million million.
BND	Brunei, dollar (international currency symbol)
BNM	Banco Nacional de Mexico. National Bank of Mexico.
BNO	Bank of New Orleans
BNP	Banque Nationale de Paris. National Bank of Paris.
B of NS	Bank of Nova Scotia
BNU	Banco Nacional Ultramarino. Overseas National Bank, Portugal.
BNZ	Bank of New Zealand
BO	broker's order
BO	brought over
BO	buyer's option
BOAD	Banque Ouest Africaine de Développement. West African Development Bank. BOAD aims to promote balanced development of the member states of the West African Monetary Union and to achieve West African economic integration. Members are Benin, Burkina Faso, Côte d'Ivoire, Guinea–Bissau, Mali, Niger, Senegal, and Togo.
BOB	Bolivia, boliviano (international currency symbol)
BOB	Bureau of the Budget
BOBA	British Overseas Banks' Association
BOBL	*Bundesobligation*. German government five-year bond in which derivatives are also traded.

BOBS	Board of Banking Supervision
BOCE	Board of Customs and Excise
BofE	Bank of England
BOGOF	buy one get one free. Employee share ownership scheme in the UK in which for each share in their company purchased by an employee he or she is given one free.
BOJ	Bank of Japan. Central bank of Japan which manages monetary policy and issues currency, and acts as lender as last resort.
BOLSA	Bank of London and South America
BOMA	Building Owners and Managers Association. Based in Washington, DC with subsidiaries throughout the USA, providing programmes, products, and services to individuals and organizations dealing in commercial and multi-unit residential property management services.
BONUS	borrower's option for notes and underwritten standby
BOP	balance of payments. Balance of a national account in which all payments of money are recorded during a certain period. BOP is divided between current and capital accounts.
BOS	business operating system
BOT	balance of trade. Difference between a country's exports and imports.
BOT	Board of Trade, *now* part of Department of Trade and Industry (**DTI**)
BOTB	British Overseas Trade Board
BOVESPA	Bolsa de Valores de São Paulo. Largest of Brazil's nine stock exchanges. The BOVESPA is the most widely quoted share index in Brazil.
BP	basis point
BP	bills payable
BPAC	budget programme activity code
BPAY	bill(s) payable
BPB	bank post bills
BPB	blanket position bond
BPC	British Productivity Council
BPD	barrels (of oil) per day
BPD	Bureau of the Public Debt
BPS	Basis point, *also* **BIPS**

BQA	British Quality Association
BR	bank rate
BR	bank robber(y)
BR	bill receivable
BRC	Brazilian cruzeiro (*former* currency; not used since 1993, *now* real)
BRC	British Retail Consortium
BRD	Brunei dollar (international currency symbol)
BREC	bills receivable
BRI	Banque des Règlements Internationaux. Bank for International Settlements.
BRL	Brazil, real (international currency symbol)
BROU	Banco de la Republica Oriental des Uruguay. Bank of the Oriental Republic of Uruguay.
BS	bill of sale
BS	bill of store
BSA	Building Societies' Association
BSC	Building Societies Commission. UK body, formerly responsible for supervising and administering the system of regulation of building societies. These duties were taken over by the Financial Services Authority (**FSA**) in 2001.
B Sc (Econ.)	
	Bachelor of Science in Economics
BSD	Bahamas, dollar (international currency symbol)
BSE	Bombay Stock Exchange
BSE	Boston Stock Exchange
BSE	Brussels Stock Exchange
BSEC	Black Sea Economic Co-operation Group. Founded in 1992 to promote economic cooperation in the region. Priority areas of interest include: transport and communications, energy, environmental protection, tourism, trade and industrial cooperation, agriculture and agro-industry, healthcare and pharmaceuticals, science and technology, and finance administration. Members are Albania, Armenia, Azerbaijan, Bulgaria, Georgia, Greece, Moldova, Romania, Russia, Turkey, and Ukraine. Austria, Egypt, Israel, Italy, Poland, Slovakia, and Tunisia are observers.
B share	Class of ordinary share with full voting rights. Often reserved for original owners as a means of keeping control of the company in their hands.

BSI	British Standards Institute. UK authority that publishes the national standards for industrial and consumer products. The majority of the work it carries out is internationally linked. The Institute has a certification trade mark, the "kitemark".
BSI	Building Societies' Institute
BSIA	British Security Industries Association
BSIS	Business Sponsorship Incentive Scheme
BSO	Business Statistics Office
BSP	business systems planning
BSS	Business Start-up Scheme
BST	bulk supply tariff
B of T	Bank of Tokyo
BTAP	bond trade analysis programme
BTC	Bankers' Trust Company (US)
BTG	British Technology Group. Formed in 1981 by the merger of the National Enterprise Board (**NEB**) and the National Research and Development Corporation (**NRDC**).
BTI	British Trade International
BTM	book to market. The ratio of book value to market value of equity.
BTN	Bhutan ngultrum (currency)
BTN	Brussels Tariff Nomenclature. Replaced by Customs Co-operation Council Nomenclature (**CCCN**) and then by Harmonized System Nomenclature (**HSN**). A six-digit harmonized commodity description and coding system of statistics.
BTP	*buono tesoro poliennali*. Italian government bonds of 5–10 year maturities, mostly 10-year maturity.
BTR	Bhutan, rupee (international currency symbol)
BU	break-up
BU	bushel(s)
Buba	Bundesbank. Central Bank of Germany.
BUDFIN	Budget and Finance Division (NATO)
BUK	Burmese kyat (currency)
BUX Index	Budapest Stock Exchange share price index
BV	*Besloten Venootschap*. Netherlands private limited company.
BV	book value

BVCA   British Venture Capital Association. Association representing the major suppliers of venture capital which invest principally in the UK.

BVL 30 Index
               Lisbon Stock Exchange main share price index

BWP   Botswana, pula (international currency symbol)

BYR   Belarus, ruble (international currency symbol)

BZD   Belize, dollar (international currency symbol)

BZ$ Belize dollar divided into 100 cents

C

¢	Costa Rican colón divided into 100 céntimos (currency)
¢	El Salvador colón divided into 100 centavos (currency)
¢	Ghana cedi (currency)
©	copyright
£c	Cyprus pound divided into 100 cents (currency)
C$	Canadian dollar divided into 100 cents (currency)
C$	Nicaraguan córdoba divided into 100 centavos (currency)
CA	capital account. Banking and investment brokerage term for accounts that hold a significant proportion of an organization's or investor's wealth.
CA	capital allowance
CA	capital appreciation. Banking term for return on investment or primary capital.
CA	capital asset
CA	cash account
CA	Chartered Accountant. US certification of competency in accounting. Less rigorous than Certified Public Accountant.
CA	Chartered Accountant. Member of the Institute of Chartered Accountants of Scotland.
CA	chief accountant
CA	controller of accounts
CA	cost account. Accounting and general business term for account established for direct costs associated with production.
CA	cost accountant. Accounting term for personnel responsible for determining costs of items involved in production.
CA	credit account. Banking and accounting term for account established in which credit can be drawn up to a specified amount.
CA	Crown Agent. Member of a board appointed by the Minister of Overseas Development to provide services for a number of overseas governments and international organizations. (UK)

CA   current account. Banking and accounting term for account with ongoing activity.

CA   current assets

C/A   *cuenta abierta*. Open account. (Spain)

Ca   *compagnia* (Italy), *conpanhia* (Portugal), *compañia* (Spain). Company.

CAA   Capital Allowances Act

CAAT   computer aided/assisted audit technique

CABA   Charge Account Bankers' Association

CABEI   Central American Bank for Economic Integration. Banco Centroamericano de Integracion Economico (BCIE).

CABMA   Canadian Association of British Manufacturers and Agencies

CAC   Central Arbitration Committee (US)

CAC   Compagnie des Agents de Change. French stockbrokers' association.

CAC   Cotation Assistée en Continue. Electronic trading system used on the Paris Bourse, introduced in 1988.

CAC-40 index
     Compagnie des Agents de Change 40 Index. Blue chip index of the Paris Stock Exchange. (France)

CACDS   Centre for Advanced Computing and Decision Support

CACM   Central American Common Market

CAD   Canada, dollar (international currency symbol)

CAD   cash against disbursements

CAD   cash against documents

CAD   Comité d'Aide au Développment. Development Assistance Committee. (France)

CADPOS   communications and data processing operating system

CAE   Certified Association Executive. Designation conferred by the American Society of Association Executives following a course of study designed to enhance all round competency in the field of association management.

CAE   *Cobrese al entregar*. Cash on delivery. (Spain)

CAEA   Central American Economics Association

CAEC   Central American Economic Community

CAEM   Conseil d'Assistance Économique Mutuelle. Council for Mutual Economic Aid (France). *See* **COMECON**.

CAES	Computer Assisted Execution System (US)
CAF	Charities Aid Foundation/Fund
CAF	clerical, administrative, and fiscal
CAF	cost, assurance, and freight
CAF	*coût, assurance, fret.* Cost, assurance, freight. (France)
CAFAO	Customs and Fiscal Assistance Office. Established in 1996, this Taxation and Customs Union programme of the European Commission in Bosnia-Hercegovina aims to facilitate the implementation of the customs-related provision of the Dayton/Paris Peace Agreements.
CAFE	corporate average fuel economy. Fuel consumption standard for automobiles. (US)
CAFM	commercial air freight movement
CAFO	command accounting and finance office
CAFOD	Catholic Fund for Overseas Development
CAFR	comprehensive annual financial report
CAGR	compound annual growth rate
CAIB	Certified Associate of the Institute of Bankers
CALD	calculated
CALG	calculating
CALN	calculation
CAMEL	C – capital adequacy, A – asset quality, M – management quality, E – earnings and L – liquidity. Five main areas which are examined by Bank supervisory bodies.
CAMPS	Cumulative Auction Market Preferred Stocks
CAN	customs assigned numbers
CAN$	Canadian dollar
CAO	Central Accounting Officer
CAO	Chief Accounting Officer
CAP	capitalization
CAP	Common Agricultural Policy. Policy of the European Union for assisting the farm sector. The main aims of the CAP are fair living standards for farmers and an improvement in agricultural efficiency. The CAP is administered by the European Agricultural Guidance and Guarantee Fund (**EAGGF**), with major policy and operational decisions (e.g. the fixing of annual farm prices) residing in the hands of the Council of Ministers of the EU.

CAPA	Canadian Association of Purchasing Agents
CAPM	capital assets pricing model
CAPM	Certificate in Advanced Property Marketing
CAPS	Cashiers' Automatic Processing System
CAPS	Convertible Adjustable Preferred Stock. Preferred stock, with an adjustable interest rate pegged to US Treasury security rates, that can be exchanged, during the period after the announcement of each dividend rate for the next period, for common stock or cash with a market value equal to the par value of the stock.
CAR	compounded annual rate/return (of interest)
CARE	Cottage and Rural Enterprises
CARIBANK	Caribbean Development Bank
CARICOM	Caribbean Community. The Treaty of Chaguaramas, establishing the Caribbean Community and Common Market, was signed by the Prime Ministers of Barbados, Guyana, Jamaica, and Trinidad and Tobago at Chaguaramas, Trinidad, on 4 July 1973, and entered into force on 1 August 1973. Members are Antigua and Barbuda, Bahamas, Barbados, Belize, Dominica, Grenada, Guyana, Jamaica, Montserrat, St Kitts and Nevis, St Vincent and the Grenadines, Suriname, and Trinidad and Tobago. Anguilla, the British Virgin Islands, and Turks and Caicos Islands are associate members. Haiti is a provisional member. CARICOM has three areas of activity: (i) economic cooperation through the Caribbean Common Market; (ii) coordination of foreign policy; (iii) functional cooperation in areas such as health, education, and culture, labour and manpower development, and women's affairs.
CARIFTA	Caribbean Free Trade Area/Association, *now* **CARICOM**
CARIPLO	Cassa du Risparmio delle Provincie Lombarde. Savings Bank of the Province of Lombardy, Italy.
CART	Community Action to Promote Rural Tourism (EU)
CA(SA)	Chartered Accountant (South Africa)
CASAO	Chartered Accountants Students' Association of Ontario
CASB	Cost Accounting Standards Board
CASH	cashier
CASOE	computer accounting system for office expenditures
CASU	Cooperative Association of Suez Canal Users
CAT	Certified Accounting Technician

CAT	charges, access, terms (pensions)
CAT	computer-assisted trading
CATA	Commonwealth Association of Tax Administration
CATS	Certificate of Accrual on Treasury Securities. Investment term for document of accrued earnings on US Treasury securities
CATS	Computer-Assisted Trading System. CATS allows entry and automatic execution of orders and carries market information on the Toronto Stock Exchange.

CAT standards
Charges, Access, and Terms. Voluntary standards for charges, access, and terms published by the Treasury. (UK)

CB	cash book
CB	Census Bureau (US)
CB	cost/benefit
CB	country bill
C-B	Creditanstalt-Bankverein. Credit Institution and Bank Association. Austria's largest banking institution.
CB	currency bond
CBA	Certified Bank Auditor. Certification offered by the Bank Administration Institute.
CBA	Certified Business Appraiser. Certification offered by the Institute of Business Appraisers to those meeting established education and practice standards for appraising the value of a business.
CBA	Commercial Bank of Australia
CBA	cost/benefit analysis. General business term for quantitative and qualitative analysis of factors involved in a proposed venture.
CBAO	Community Bankers Association of Oklahoma (US)
CBB	commercial blanket bond
CBC	Citizens Budget Commission (New York)
CBC	Commonwealth Banking Corporation
CBCM	cheque book-charging method
CBCS	Commonwealth Bureau of Census and Statistics (Australia)
CBCT	customer–bank communication terminal
CBD	cash before delivery. General business term specifying that payment is required before the vendor will make delivery.

CBE	Certified Bank Examiner. Professional certification by American Bankers' Association.
CBF	central board of finance
CBI	Confederation of British Industry. UK organization that represents the collective interests of member companies in dealings with government and trade unions.
CBK	cheque book
CB/L	commercial bill of lading
CBNY	Chemical Bank, New York
CBO	Collateralized Bond Obligation
CBO	Congressional Budget Office (US)
CBOE	Chicago Board Options Exchange. Options exchange established in 1973.
CBOT	Chicago Board of Trade. Commodity market, first established in 1848. The CBOT began as a trading centre for grain and quickly became a centre for futures dealing, instituting the first contract in 1951. *Also* CBT.
CBR	Certified Buyer Representative
CBRS	Canadian Bond Rating Service
CBSI	Chartered Building Societies Institute
CBT	Connecticut Bank and Trust
CBU	Clearing Banks Union
CC	cash credit
CC	Chamber of Commerce
CC	Charity Commission
CC	civil commotion (insurance)
CC	Competition Commission, *formerly* the Monopolies and Mergers Commission (**MMC**)
CC	*compte courant*. Current account. (France)
CC	continuation clause
CC	*conto corrente*. Current account. (Italy)
CC	contra credit
CC	country cheque/clearing
CC	credit card
CCA	Consumer Credit Act, 1974 (UK)

CCA   current cost accounting. Accounting method which records a company's costs and revenues after taking into account changes in prices affecting those items and the value of assets at current replacement cost.

CCAB   Canadian Circulations Audit Board

CCAB   Consultative Committee of Accountancy Bodies. Major accountancy bodies in the UK and Ireland first joined together in 1974 to form the CCAB. It provides a forum in which matters affecting the profession as a whole can be discussed and coordinated and enables the profession to speak with a unified voice to the government.

CCBS   California Canadian Banks

CCBS   Centre for Central Banking Studies

CCC   Commercial Credit Corporation

CCC   Commodity Credit Corporation, a US government-owned corporation established in 1933 to stabilize and support farm income and prices

ccc   *cwmni cyfyngedig cyhoeddus*. Public limited company. (Wales)

CCCN   Customs Cooperation Council Nomenclature, *formerly* Brussels Tariff Nomenclature (**BTN**), *now* Harmonized System Nomenclature (**HSN**)

CCCS   Consumer Credit Counseling Services

CCE   current cash equivalent

CCEI   composite cost effectiveness index

CCH   commercial clearing house

CCI   Chamber of Commerce and Industry

CCIA   Consumer Credit Insurance Association (US)

CCIFP   Chambre de Compensation des Instruments Financiers de Paris. Clearing house for the Marché à Terme des Instrument Financiers (**MATIF**), the French financial futures exchange.

CCIM   Certified Commercial Investment Member. CCIMs are recognized experts in commercial real estate brokerage, leasing, asset management valuation, and investment analysis.

CCIPD   Companion of the Chartered Institute of Personnel and Development. Companionship is gained by invitation only and awarded in recognition of significant contribution to the profession or the Institute.

CCL   contingent credit lines (**IMF**)

CCN   command control number

CCO	country clearing office
CCP	Central Counterparty
CCP	*conto corrent postale*. Current postal account. (Italy)
CCP	credit card purchase
CCR	credit card reader
CCRB	Cooperatif Centraal Raiffeisen-Boerenleenbank. Raiffeisen's Central Cooperative Farmers' Loan Bank, the Netherlands.
CCRT	Check Collectors Round Table
CCS	cross currency swap
CCSB	Credit Card Service Bureau
CCSR	cash-to-common-stock ratio
CCT	Common Customs Tariff, replaced by Combined Nomenclature (**CN**)
CCUL	California Credit Union League
CC US	Chamber of Commerce of the United States
CD	carried down
CD	cash discount
CD	certificate of deposit. Negotiable instrument issued by a bank that shows that cash was deposited at a certain rate of interest for a period of up to five years.
CD	consular declaration
CD	cum dividend. With dividend.
CD	customs declaration
C/D	carried down
CDB	Caribbean Development Bank. Established to contribute to the economic growth and development of the member countries of the Caribbean and promote economic cooperation and integration among them, with particular regard to the needs of the less developed countries.
CDC	Commonwealth Development Corporation
CDF	Congo-Kinshasa, Congolese franc (international currency symbol)
CDFC	Commonwealth Development Finance Company
CD FWD	carried forward
CDI	**CREST** Depositary Interests
CDIC	Canada Deposit Insurance Corporation

CDipAF Certified Diploma in Accounting and Finance (from **ACCA**)

CDIP F & A

Certified Diploma in Finance and Accounting

C Div cum dividend. With dividend.

CDN Canadian Dealing Network. The organized **OTC** market of Canada, a subsidiary of the Toronto Stock Exchange.

CDNX Canadian Venture Exchange. Amalgamation of Vancouver and Alberta stock exchanges.

CDR Casa di Risparmio. Savings Bank. (Italy)

CDS credit default swap

CDV Commonwealth dollar value

CDW collision damage waiver (US)

CE *caveat emptor.* Let the buyer beware.

CE Chancellor of the Exchequer

CE chief executive

CE cost effectiveness. General business term for concept of soundness of plans and practices based on direct and indirect costs versus income.

C&E Customs and Excise. Board formed in UK in 1909 to manage duties (customs) on imported and exported goods and services and (excise) on home-produced goods and services. It also administers **VAT**.

CEA Certificate of Estate Agency

CEA Comité européen des assurances. European Insurance Committee. (France)

CEA Commodity Exchange Act/Authority

CEA Council of Economic Advisers (US)

CEC Centre for Economic Cooperation (UN)

CEC Commission of the European Communities

CEC Commodities Exchange Center. Based in New York, the location of five futures exchanges: **COMEX**, **CSCE**, **NYMEX**, **NYCE**, and **NYFE**.

CECC Communauté Européene de Crédit Communal. European Municipal Credit Community.

CECD Communauté Européene du charbon et de l'acier. European Coal and Steel Community. (France)

CED Council for Economic Development (US)

CEDA Committee for Economic Development of Australia

CEDEL   Centrale de Livraison de Valeurs Mobilières. Settlement system for **Eurobond** trading, established in Luxembourg in 1970. CEDEL is both a clearing house and an agency for dividend collection.

CEDEX   *courrier d'enterprise à distribution exceptionelle.* Special business post code. (France)

CEDRIC   Customs and Excise Department Reference and Information Computer

CEE   Commission Économique pour l'Europe. Economic Commission for Europe.

CEEAC   Communauté Économique des États de l'Afrique Centrale. Economic Community of Central African States. The CEEAC was established in 1983 to promote regional economic co-operation and to establish a Central African Common Market. Members are Burundi, Cameroon, Central African Republic, Chad, Democratic Republic of the Congo, Republic of the Congo, Equatorial Guinea, Gabon, Rwanda, São Tomé e Príncipe. Observer: Angola.

CEEC   Council for European Economic Cooperation

CeFiMS   Centre for Financial and Management Studies (University of London)

CEFTA   Central European Free Trade Association. Established in 1992 to set up a free trade area and now consisting of Poland, Hungary, Czech Republic, Romania, Bulgaria, Slovakia, and Slovenia.

CEGB   Central Electricity Generating Board (UK)

CEI   Central European Initiative. Austria, Hungary, Italy, and Yugoslavia met in November 1989 on Italy's initiative to form an economic and political cooperation group in the region. Members are Albania, Austria, Belarus, Bosnia-Hercegovina, Bulgaria, Croatia, Czech Republic, Hungary, Italy, Macedonia, Moldova, Poland, Romania, Slovakia, Slovenia, and Ukraine.

CEI   cost-effectiveness index

CEIR   Corporation for Economic and Industrial Research

CEIS   Cost and Economic Information System

CELA   Council for Exports to Latin America

CELEX   *Communitatis Europeae Lex.* European Community Law.

CEM   cost and effectiveness method

CEMA   Council for Economic Mutual Assistance. *See* **COMECON**.

CeMAP	Certificate in Mortgage Advice and Practice
CEMLA	Centro de Estudios Monetarios Latino-americanos. Latin-American Centre for Monetary Studies.
CENT	centavo
CENT	centesimo
CENT	centime
CEO	chief executive officer
CER	closer economic relationship
CERT INV	certified invoice
CES	cost-effectiveness study
CES	cost-estimating system
CESR	Committee of European Securities Regulators, *formerly* **FESCO**
CET	common external tariff
CETF	capital element tax free
CEUSA	Committee for Exports to the United States of America
CEX	Corn Exchange Bank
CF	Comoran franc (currency)
CF	compensation fee
CF	cost and freight
C/F	carried forward
CFA	cash-flow accounting. Accounting system that considers only cash and does not deduct non-cash items such as depreciation.
CFA	Chartered Financial Analyst. Established in 1962 in the USA, CFA is a globally recognized credential for investment analysis and advice. It is overseen and administered by the Association for Investment Management and Research (**AIMR**).
CF & A	Chief of Finance and Accounting (US)
CFA	Communauté financière Africaine. African Financial Community, as in CFA franc. *See* **XAF**; **XOF**.
CFAE	Council for Financial Aid to Education
CFAT	cash flow after taxes
CFB	Consumer Fraud Bureau (US)
CFB	Council of Foreign Bondholders

CFC	Common Fund for Commodities (US)
CFCE	Conseil des fédérations commerciales d'Europe. Council of European Commercial Federations.
CFD	contract for difference. A derivative product.
CFD	Corporate Finance Director. Common job title for a corporate officer responsible for financial planning and recordkeeping.
CFE	Certified Financial Examiner. Professional certification from the Society of Financial Examiners.
CFI	Corporacion Financiera Internacional. International Finance Corporation. (Spain)
CFI	cost, freight, and insurance
CFI	Court of First Instance (EU)
CFMA	Central Financial Management Activities
CFO	Chief Financial Officer. Common job title for a corporate officer responsible for handling funds, signing checks over a certain amount, financial planning, and recordkeeping.
CFOD	Catholic Fund for Overseas Development
CFP	Certified Financial Planner. Professional designation offered by the Certified Financial Planner Board of Standards, to candidates who pass a comprehensive exam.
CFP	Common Fisheries Policy (EU)
CFP	Communauté financière du Pacifique. Pacific Financial Community, as in CFP franc.
CFr	Congolese franc (currency)
CFS	Certified Finance Specialist
CFSA	Certified Financial Services Auditor (US)
CFSP	Common Foreign and Security Policy (EU)
CFSR	Commission on Financial Structure and Regulation (White House)
CFTC	Commodity Futures Trading Commission. US federal regulatory agency established in 1974 that administers the Commodity Exchange Act. The CFTC monitors the futures and options on futures markets in the US and protects market participants against manipulation, abusive trade practices, and fraud.
CFTC	Commonwealth Fund for Technical Cooperation
CFY	Company Fiscal Year. Accounting and general business term referring to the calendar by which a business's fiscal year begins and ends.

CFY	Current Fiscal Year. Accounting and general business term designating an event as occurring during the present financial accounting year.
CGA	cargo's proportion of general average
CGA	certified general accountant
CGAP	Certified Government Auditing Professional (US)
CGBR	central government borrowing requirement
CGHB	Cape of Good Hope Bank (South Africa)
CGHSB	Cape of Good Hope Savings Bank (South Africa)
CGO	Central Gilts Office
CGPS	Canadian Government Purchasing System
CGT	capital gains tax. Tax in UK on a realized increase in the value of a capital asset. Capital gains are subject to capital gains tax (CGT). The tax does not cover gains arising from the sale of personal belongings, including cars or principal dwelling houses, but it does cover gains from the sale of stock exchange securities.
Ch$	Chile, peso (currency)
CHANGE	stock exchange
CHAPS	Clearing House Automated Payments Systems. CHAPS provides instant clearing for electronic transfers.
CHAT MTG	chattel mortgage
CHF	Switzerland, franc (international currency symbol)
ChFC	Chartered Financial Consultant. Financial planning professional designation awarded by the American College of the American Society of Chartered Life Underwriters. Requirements include successful completion of a 10-course programme and three years' professional experience.
CHGD	charged
CHIPS	Clearing House Interbank Payments Systems. Computerized clearing network system for transfer of international dollar payments and settlement of interbank foreign exchange obligations.
CHOGMs	Commonwealth Heads of Government Meetings
CH PD	charges paid
CH PPD	charges prepaid
CHQ	cheque

CH of S   Chamber of Shipping

CHS   charges on account

CI   consular invoice

C&I   cost and insurance

CI$ Cayman Island dollar divided into 100 cents

CIA   cash in advance

CIA   Certified Internal Auditor. International certification awarded by the Institute of Internal Auditors (IIA) that reflects competence in the principles and practices of internal auditing.

Cia   *compagnia* (Italy), *companhia* (Portugal), *compañia* (Spain). Company.

CIAT   Centro Interamericao de Administradores Tributarios. Inter-American Centre of Revenue Administration.

CIB   Californian Independent Bankers (US)

CIB   Chartered Institute of Bankers (UK)

CIB   Corporation of Insurance Brokers

CIBC   Canadian Imperial Bank of Commerce

CIBOR   Copenhagen Interbank Offered Rate. Rate available to banks and savings banks depositing three-month uncollateralized kroner with a prime bank. (Denmark)

CIC   Capital Issues Committee

CIC   Chartered Investment Counselor (US)

CICA   Canadian Institute of Chartered Accountants. National membership organization of Chartered Accountants of Canada.

CICA   Confédération Internationale du Crédit Agricole. International Confederation for Agricultural Credit.

CICA   Criminal Injuries Compensation Authority (UK)

CICAP   Criminal Injuries Compensation Appeals Panel (UK)

CICG   Centre Internationale du Commerce de Gros. International Centre for Wholesale Trade.

CICP   Centre for International Crime Prevention (UN)

CICP   Confédération Internationale du Crédit Populaire. International Confederation for Small-Scale Credit.

CID   Council for Industrial Design

CIDE   Comision de Inversion y Desarrollo Economico. Commission for Investment and Economic Development. (Uruguay)

CIDESA Centre International de Documentation Économique et Sociale Africaine. International Centre for African Social and Economic Documentation.

Cie *companie*. Company. (France)

CIET Centro Interamericano de Estudios Tributarios. Inter-American Centre of Revenue Studies.

CIF, CI&F cost, insurance, and freight

CIFAS Credit Industry Fraud Avoidance System (UK)

CIF&C cost, insurance, freight, and commission

CIFC&I cost, insurance, freight, commission, and interest

CIF&E cost, insurance, freight, and exchange

CIF&I cost, insurance, freight, and interest

CIFLT cost, insurance, and freight, London terms

CII Chartered Insurance Institute. Professional association, founded in 1873, for individuals engaged in insurance. It is the largest professional and educational body in insurance and financial services in the world. The objects of the Institute are to promote efficiency in insurance, to foster improvement in insurance practice, and to provide information and education in insurance. (UK)

CILA Chartered Institute of Loss Adjusters. Professional Association, founded in 1942, to set standards and rules for, and provide information to, loss adjusters.

CIM Chartered Institute of Marketing

CIMA Chartered Institute of Management Accountants (UK)

CIMC Certified Investment Management Consultant. Designation from the Institute for Investment Management Consultants to members who pass an examination and have at least three years of professional financial consulting experience.

CIMgt Companion of the Institute of Management

CIMS Certified Investment Management Specialist. Designation from the Institute for Investment Management to associate members who pass an examination and meet work-experience requirements.

CINB & T Continental Illinois National Bank and Trust

CIOBS Chartered Institute of Bankers in Scotland

CIOT Chartered Institute of Taxation

CIP capital investment program

CIP common industrial policy (EU)

CIP	Cost Improvement Proposal
CIPD	Chartered Institute of Personnel and Development. The Chartered Institute of Personnel and Development has over 105,000 members and is the leading professional institute for those involved in the management and development of people.
CIPFA	Chartered Institute of Public Finance and Accountancy (UK)
CIPS	Certified International Property Specialist. Professional certification from the National Association of Realtors. Many realtors work with buyers and sellers from different countries or cultures.
CIPS	Chartered Institute of Purchasing and Supply
CIR	Commissioners of Inland Revenue
CIR	cost information report
CIRA	Conference of Industrial Research Associations
CIRIEC	Centre International de Recherches et d'Information sur l'Économie Collective. International Centre of Research and Information on Collective Economy.
CIS	cost inspection service
CISA	Canadian Industrial Safety Association
CISA	Centro Italiano Studi Aziendali. Italian Centre for Business Studies.
CISCO	City Group for Smaller Companies (UK)
CISL	Confederation Internationale des Syndicats Libres. International Confederation of Free Trade Unions. (France)
CISL	Confederazione Italiana Sindicati Lavoratori. Italian Confederation of Workers' Trade Unions.
CITB	Construction Industry Training Board
CITIC	China International Trust and Investment Corporation. Chinese organization issuing bonds to finance joint ventures in China.
CJEU	Court of Justice of the European Union
C/L	cash letter
CLC	Canadian Labour Congress
CLC	Chartered Life Underwriter of Canada
CLCB	Committee of London Clearing Banks
CLD	called (stock exchange)
CLD	cancelled

CLD	cleared
CLG	company limited by guarantee
CLI	cost-of-living index
CLO	Certified Leasing Officer
CLP	Chile, peso (international currency symbol)
CLS	Continuous Linked Settlement
CLSB	Committee of London and Scottish Bankers
CLU	Chartered Life Underwriter
CM	Common Market
CMA	Certificate in Management Accountancy. Certificate of the Institute of Cost and Executive Accountants issued to a Member, Fellow, or Associate who holds the position of financial executive, controller, or director of a standing organization approved by the Council.
CMA	Certificate of Management Accounting (USA)
CMA	Certified Management Accountant. Title awarded by the Institute of Management Accountants (**IMA**) to persons meeting certain basic requirements, principally passing an examination covering economic theory, financial management, cost accounting, etc.
CMA	Cost and Management Accountant (New Zealand)
CMB	Chase Manhattan Bank
CMBA	Connecticut Mortgage Bankers' Association (US)
CMBS	commercial mortgage backed securities
CMC	Certified Management Consultant
CMCA	Certified Manager of Community Associations
CME	Chicago Mercantile Exchange. Established in 1919 as a commodity futures market. In 1972 CME developed the international monetary market in which currency futures were initiated.
CMEA	*see* **COMECON**
CMHC	Central Mortgage and Housing Corporation (Canada)
CML	Council of Mortgage Lenders
CMLA	Colorado Mortgage Lenders' Association (US)
CMMA	clothing monetary maintenance allowance
CMO	collateralized mortgage obligation. Type of mortgage-backed bond that separates mortgage pools into two maturity classes called tranches: companion bonds, and planned amortization

class bonds. CMOs generally give investors a higher level of security than other mortgage-backed securities. (US)

CMP   cost of maintaining project

CM PF   cumulative preference/preferred shares

CMS   constant maturity swap

CN   Combined Nomenclature: an 8-digit goods nomenclature that replaces the **CCT** and **NIMEXE** nomenclatures. It is updated annually (EU)

C/N   credit note

CNAR   compound net annual rate

CNB   Crocker National Bank

CNC   Conseil National de la Comptabilité. National Council of Accountancy. (France)

CNIEC   Chinese National Import and Export Corporation

CNIPA   Committee of National Institutes of Patent Agents

CNMV   Comisión Nacional del Mercado de Valores. National Capital Market Commission. Regulatory body of the Madrid Stock Exchange.

CNNC   Chinese National Nonferrous Metals Corporation. Organization established in 1983 and based in Beijing. It manages a portion of China's nonferrous metals imports and exports.

CNT   Confederación Nacional de Trabajo. National Federation of Labour. (Spain)

CNY   China, yuan renminbi (international currency symbol)

CO   *compte ouvert*. Open account. (France)

C/O   carried over

C/O   cash order

Co   company

COB   close of business

COB   Commission des Opérations de Bourse. Supervisory body for the French stock exchange, established in 1967. Belgium has a similar organization with a similar name.

COBOL   common business-oriented language (computing)

COBRA   Congressional Omnibus Budget Reconciliation Act. US federal legislation that gives employees the right to carry their group health insurance coverage for up to 18 months after leaving the employer, by paying the full premium. The advantage to the employee is that the full premium of the group policy is generally lower than the individual rate on comparable coverage.

CoC	Chamber of Commerce
CoCoA	continuously contemporary accounting
COD	cargo on desk
COD	cash/collect on delivery
CODA	cash or deferred arrangement (US, pensions)
CODOT	Classification of Occupations and Directory of Occupational Titles. Introduced in the UK in 1972. Replaced by the Standard Occupational Classification (**SOC**).
COEA	cost and operational effectiveness analysis
COFACE	Compagnie Français pour l'Assurance du Commerce Extérieur. French export credit guarantee system.
CofB	confirmation of balance
COGS	cost of goods sold
COH	cash on hand
COI	certificate of origin and interest
CoID	Council of Industrial Design
COIE	Council of Invisible Exports
COIN-OP	coin-operated
COINS	Committee on Improvement of National Statistics (US)
Col$	Colombian peso (currency)
COLA	cost-of-living adjustment. Clause in employment contracts. (US)
COLA	cost-of-living allowance
COLC	Cost of Living Council
COLI	Cost of Living Index. US government statistic, generally referred to as Consumer Price Index.
COLL	collateral, *also* COLLAT
COM	commission
COMBS	Contracted-out mixed benefit scheme (UK, pensions)
COMDEV	Commonwealth Development Finance Company
COMECON	Council for Mutual Economic Aid/Assistance (*also* CMEA). The major international organization of the socialist countries aimed at multilateral cooperation and integration in economic, scientific, and technical fields. Founded in 1949, COMECON finally collapsed in 1991 after the revolutions in eastern Europe.

COMESA Common Market for Eastern and Southern Africa. COMESA was established in 1994 and is an African economic grouping of 20 member states who are committed, over the long term, to the creation of a Common Market for Eastern and Southern Africa.

COMETT Community Action Programme in Education and Training for Technology (EU)

COMEX Commodity Exchange of New York. Major commodity market in metals, established in 1970, dealing principally in futures contracts.

COMO Committee of Marketing Organizations

COMP CURR
Comptroller of the Currency

COMP-GEN
Comptroller-General

COMPS contracted-out money purchase scheme (UK, pensions)

COMPTR comptroller

CON CR contra credit

CON INV consular invoice

CONSOB Commissione Nazionale per le Società e la Borsa. Instituted in 1974 as the supervisory body for the Italian stock exchange.

CONSOLS Consolidated Funds. Right to a perpetual annuity/annual payment of interest (since 1905, 2.5 per cent) but can be sold at a price reflecting yield in comparable securities.

CONTBD contraband

CONV convertible

COO Chief Operating Officer. Common US job title for corporate officer responsible for day-to-day operations of the organization.

COOC contact with oil or other cargo (insurance)

COP Colombia, peso (international currency symbol)

CoR Committee of the Regions (EU)

COREPER Committee of Permanent Representatives (EU)

CORES computer-assisted order routing and execution system, Tokyo Stock Exchange

CORP corporation (US)

COS cash on shipment

COSA	cost of sales adjustment
CoSIRA	Council of Small Industries in Rural Area (UK)
COSRS	contracted-out salary-related scheme (UK, pensions)
COWPS	Council of Wages and Price Stability (US)
CP	carriage paid
CP	charter party
CP	commercial paper. Unsecured note issued by companies for short-term borrowing purposes.
CP	concert party
CPA	Certified Practising Accountant (Australia)
CPA	Certified Public Accountant. Conferred by a US state or similar governmental jurisdiction and authorizes the holder to practise as a certified public accountant in that jurisdiction.
CPA	Certified Public Accountant. Person holding an official certificate as an accountant, having fulfilled all legal and licensing requirements at the state level and with the **AICPA**. Also a qualification from the Institute of Certified Public Accountants in Ireland.
CPA	cost planning and appraisal
CPA	critical path analysis
CPB	casual payments book
CPC	Competition Policy Co-ordination (**OFT**)
CPD	charterers pay dues
CPD	compound
CPD	continuing professional development
CPF	contributory pension fund
CPFA	Chartered Institute of Public Finance and Accountancy (UK)
CPFF	cost plus fixed fee
CPI	consumer price index (US)
CPIF	cost plus incentive fee
CPM	Certified Property Manager. CPMs acquire valuable real estate management skills through educational courses leading to the CPM designation.
CPM	cost per thousand
CPM	Critical Path Method. Project-management technique that uses a single time estimate for each activity, the primary objective being to identify the critical path for a project.

CPO	Commodity Pool Operator. An individual or organization that operates or solicits funds for a commodity pool.
CPO	compulsory purchase order
CPP	current purchasing power
CPRC	central price regulation committee
CPS	cents per share (US)
CPT	Contador Publico Titulado. Certified Public Accountant. (Spain)
CQS	Consolidated Quote System (US)
CR	cash receipts
CR	company's risk
CR	cost reimbursement
CR	credit
CR	creditor
CR	credit rating
CR	cum rights. With rights.
CR	current rate
CRA	Canadian Resident Appraiser
CRAFTS	Central Regional Automated Funds Transfer System (US)
CRB	Certified Real Estate Brokerage manager. CRB designation is recognized as the symbol of excellence in brokerage management.
CRB	Commodity Research Bureau (US)
CRBS	customer records and billing system
CRC	Costa Rica, colón (international currency symbol)
CRCH	central register and clearing house
CRD	Central Registration Depository (UK)
CRE	Counsellor of Real Estate. The CRE is a member of the Counsellors of Real Estate, an international group of recognized professionals who provide seasoned, objective advice on real property and land-related matters.
CREA	Certified Real Estate Appraiser
CRED	credit
CRED	creditor
CRES	Certified Real Estate Specialist
CREST	UK electronic share settlement system that was introduced by CRESTCo in July 1996. CREST replaces the **TALISMAN**.

CRF	capital recovery factor
CRF	Certified in Real Estate Finance
CRND	Commissioners for the Reduction of the National Debt
CRO	Companies Registration Office. Office where the records of companies must be deposited, so as to be available to the general public.
CRP	Certified Relocation Professional
CRR	contemporaneous reserve requirements (US)
CRS	Certified Resident Specialist
CRS	computer-readable systems
CRSS	Certified Real Estate Securities Sponsor
CRT	composite rate tax
CRU	Certified Residential Underwriter
CRUs	collective reserve units. International banking currency.
Cruz	Brazilian cruzeiro (currency)
CS	capital stock
CS	Certificate in Statistics
C & S	Citizens and Southern Bank (US)
CS	*cours.* Current price. (France)
CS	credit sales
CSA	Canadian Standards Association
CSB	Central Statistical Board
CSBGM	Committee of Scottish Bank General Managers
CSBs	Canada Savings Bonds
CSBS	Conference of State Bank Supervisors (US)
CSCB	Committee of Scottish Clearing Bankers
CSCE	Coffee, Sugar, and Cocoa Exchange of New York
CSCS	Cost, Schedule, and Control System
CSE	Calcutta Stock Exchange
CSE	Cincinnati Stock Exchange
CSE	Copenhagen Stock Exchange, *formerly* **FUTOP**
CSE	Council of the Stock Exchange, London
CSF	Community support framework (EU)
CSFI	Centre for the Study of Financial Innovation
CSI	Computer Security Institute

CSIRA	Council for Small Industries in Rural Areas
CSO	Central Statistical Office, now called the Office for National Statistics (**ONS**)
CSP	Certified Sales Professional
CSP	Classification Settlement Programme. US programme in which tax examiners can offer settlements to businesses that have incorrectly classified workers (e.g. as independent contractors as opposed to full-time or part-time employees). The programme is voluntary and businesses that decline an offered settlement retain their right to appeal.
CSPI	corporate services price index
CSR	corporate social responsibility
CSRC	China Securities Regulatory Commission. Securities market regulator (China)
CT	carat, gold content
CT	corporation tax
CT	credit
CT	current
CTA	Commodity Trading Advisor. Person who, for compensation or profit, directly or indirectly offers advice on buying or selling futures or commodity options.
CTC	children's tax credit (UK)
CTCI	computer-to-computer interface
CTD	cheapest-to-deliver (bonds)
CTP	Confederación de Trabajadores del Peru. Peruvian Confederation of Labour.
CTRP	Confederación de Trabajadores de la República de Panamá. Confederation of Workers of the Republic of Panama.
CTS	centimes
CTS	cents
CTS	Consolidated Trade System. Receives and disseminates, electronically, stock last-sale prices. (US)
CTT	capital transfer tax. Tax introduced in the UK in 1975 on the transmission of wealth by gift, both during a person's lifetime and on their death. Replaced by inheritance tax (**IHT**) in 1986.
CTV	Confederación de Trabajadores de Venezuela. Confederation of Venezuelan Workers.
CU	Customs Union. Achieved in the EU on 1 July 1968.

CUA

CUA   Canadian Underwriters' Association

CULS   convertible unsecured loan stock

CUM   cumulative

CUM DIV cum divided. With dividend.

CUM PREF
cumulative preference

CUNA   Credit Union National Association

CUP   Cuba, peso (international currency symbol)

CUR   Currency

CUSIP number
Committee on Uniform Securities Identification Procedures number. Nine-digit identifier for securities traded in the US.

CUTF   Commonwealth Unit Trust Fund

CV   convertible

CVA   Certified Valuation Analyst

CVA   company voluntary arrangement

CVAS   configuration verification and accounting system

CVD   cash versus documents

CVE   Cape Verde, escudo (international currency symbol)

CVESC   Cape Verde escudo (currency)

CVL   creditors' voluntary liquidation

CVLI   cash value life insurance

CVM   Commissão de Valores Mobiliaros. Brazilian securities commission regulating the stock exchange in São Paulo.

CVP   cost-volume-profit

CWB   Central Wages Board

CWO   cash with order. Merchandise is paid for when order placed rather than when delivered.

CWPS   Council on Wages and Price Stability

CWT   Company of World Traders

CWT   hundredweight

CXT   common external tariff

CY   currency

CYP   Cyprus, pound (international currency symbol)

CZK   Czech Republic, koruna (international currency symbol)

D

D	*dogana*. Customs. (Italy)
D	*douane*. Customs. (France)
DA	deposit account (*also* D/A)
DA	discretionary account. Funds for investment with no, or only general, instructions as to how they should be invested.
D/A	days after acceptance
DAC	deductible average clause (insurance)
DAC	Development Assistance Committee (**OECD**)
DAFO	division accounting and finance office
DAGMAR	Defining Advertising Goals for Measured Advertising Response
DAP	documents against payments
DARE	demand and resource evaluation
DAS	delivered alongside ship
DAX	Deutsche Aktienindex. Share index for 30 leading equity shares quoted on the Frankfurt Stock Exchange
DB	defined benefit (pensions)
DB	Deutsche Bundesbank (German Federal Bank)
Db	dobra (currency of São Tomé e Príncipe)
D & B	Dun and Bradstreet. Organization which issues statements on the financial rating of companies. It is also a debt collecting agency.
D/B	daybook
DBA	Doctor of Business Administration
DBA	Doing Business As. Banking and general business term referring to the name of a business enterprise used in place of the owner's actual name and recorded with the country in which the business is located.
DBIU	Dominion Board of Insurance Underwriters (Canada)
DBM	Diploma in Business Management
DBMS	Data Base Management System. Group of computer software packages that integrates data in one place for sharing by all

systems on a network, allowing cross-referencing of data among files to eliminate repetition.

DBS	Development Bank of Singapore
DC	decimal classification
DC	decimal currency
DC	defined contribution (pensions)
DC	Department of Commerce
DC	documents (against) cash
D/C	deviation clause (insurance)
DCE	domestic credit expansion. Monetary aggregate that is sometimes used by the International Monetary Fund (**IMF**) in requiring monetary restraint on the part of a member country with a balance-of-payments deficit as a condition of access to the Fund's resources.
DCF	discounted cash flow. Technique used to assess profitability of capital projects which is achieved by calculating capital investments and time scales; calculating incomes from investments and time scales; and adjusting these for taxation and grant purposes. The resultant interest rate is a guide to profitability of an enterprise.
DCLAA	Developing Countries in Latin America and Asia
DCO	Dominion, Colonial and Overseas, *now* Barclays International
DCT	Department of Commerce and Trade
DCV	direct charge voucher
DD	demand draft
DD	direct debit
D/D	delivered at docks
D Day	decimal day, 15 February 1971 (UK)
DDDD	direct debit dealing day
DDR	direct debit
DE	double entry
DEA	Department of Economic Affairs, *now* disbanded (UK)
DEB	debenture
DEB	debit
DEB STK	debenture stock
D Ec	Doctor of Economics

DEC	decimal
DEC	Dollar Export Council
D Econ	Doctor of Economics
DEF	deficit
DEFL	deflation
DEM	demurrage
DEM	Germany, mark (*former* currency, *now* euro), international currency symbol
DEMUR	demurrage
DEP	deposit
DEP	depositor
DEPB	Duty Entitlement Passbook scheme. An export subsidy scheme under which any eligible exporter can apply for credits which are calculated as a percentage of the value of exported finished products.
DERM	dual exchange rate. Coexistence of a floating "financial" exchange rate and an "official" exchange rate which is normally considered fixed.
DF	dead freight
DFA	dynamic financial analysis
DFCC	Development Finance Cooperative Committee. Established under Article 325 of the 4th Lomé Convention to examine whether the objectives of financial cooperation have been attained. (EU)
DFID	Department for International Development. UK government department working to eliminate global poverty and promote sustainable development.
D F Sc	Doctor of Financial Science
DG	Directorates General. Principal bureaucratic ministers of the European Commission. (EU)
DGB	Deutscher Gewerkschaftsbund. German Trade Union Federation.
DGI	domestically generated inflation
Dh	dirham (monetary unit of United Arab Emirates)
DIDC	Depository Institutions Deregulation Committee
DIDMCA	Depository Institutions Deregulation and Monetary Decontrol Act 1980. US Act that removed interest-rate ceilings from passbook savings accounts.

DIE   designated investment exchange. Overseas investment exchange recognized by the Financial Services Authority (**FSA**).

DIG   Derivatives Implementation Group (US)

DIG   disablement income group

DIP ECON Diploma in/of Economics

DipEF   Diploma in Executive Finance, from the Institute of Cost and Executive Accountants, for executives who are not accountants

DipEMA Diploma in Executive and Management Accountancy, granted by the Institute of Cost and Executive Accountants and restricted to Fellows of the Institute who must also pass the Diploma Examination

DipFM   Diploma in Financial Management

DipFS   Diploma in Financial Services

DIR   Directive. **EU** member states must implement in national laws.

DISB   disbursement

DISC   discount

DISC   Domestic International Sales Corporation (US)

DISCT   discount

DIT   double income tax

DITB   Distributive Industry Training Board

DIV   divide

DIV   division

DIVDE   *dividende*. Dividend. (French)

DIVI   dividend

DIVN   division

DJF   Djibouti, franc (international currency symbol)

DJI   Dow Jones Index

DJIA   Dow Jones Industrial Average. The most widely followed stock market average, a benchmark stock average of 30 blue chip industrial stocks selected for total market value and broad public ownership and believed to reflect overall market activity. Established in 1884.

DKK   Denmark, krone (international currency symbol)

Dkr   krone (currency of Denmark and Greenland)

74

DKV	Deutsche Kassenverein. Institute which accounts for the majority of settlement and clearing in the German stock exchanges.
DL	demand loan
DL	double ledger
DLA	disability living allowance (UK)
DLS	debt liquidation scheme
DLS	dollars
DM	Deutschmark, *former* German currency, *now* euro
D-mark	Deutschmark, *former* German currency, *now* euro
DMC	direct manufacturing costs
DMFAS	debt management and financial analysis (UN)
DMO	Debt Management Office. Executive Agency of the UK Treasury that has responsibility for issuing gilts to fund the government's borrowing activities. In 2002 it took over the work of the National Investment and Loans Office (**NILO**).
DN	debit note
DNA	director of naval accounts
D NOTE	$500 note (US)
DNS	Department of National Savings
DO	deferred ordinary shares
DOC	direct operating cost
DOE	Diploma of Economics
D OEC	*Doctor Oeconomiae.* Doctor of Economics.
DOL	*Daily Official List.* The register of Securities on the main UK market and Alternative Investment Market (**AIM**) that gives the prices of trades published each day.
DOP	Dominican Republic, peso (international currency symbol)
DOS	date/day of sale
DOT	Department of the Treasury (US)
DOT	designated order turnaround. Electronic order-processing system on the New York Stock Exchange that allows members to give a limit order for stock that will be executed automatically.
DP	data processing
D/P	delivery on payment

D/P	documents against payment
DPA	deferred payment account
DPB	deposit passbook
DPC	derivative product company
DPCP	Department of Prices and Consumer Protection
DPf	pfennig, *former* German currency, *now* euro
DPI	Disposable Personal Income. Tax accounting and financial planning term for personal income not needed for basic necessities and therefore available for discretionary expenditures, such as travel, entertainment, etc.
DPP	deferred payment plan
DPS	dividend per share
DPT	deposit
DPT	distributed profit tax
DPTC	disabled person's tax credit (UK)
Dr	drachma, *former* Greek currency, *now* euro
DR	debit
DR	debtor
DR	discount rate
DR	draw
DR	drawer
DR	drawn
D/R	deposit receipt
DRC	Disability Rights Commission
DRIP	dividend reinvestment plan
DRN	drawn
DRP	dividend reinvestment plan
DRX	drachma, *former* Greek currency, *now* euro
DS	debenture stock
D Sc Econ	*Docteur en Science économiques*. Doctor of Science (Economics).
D schedule	Schedule in the UK Finance Act under which tax is levied on profits from trades and professions
DSR	debt service ratio

DSRO   Designated Self-Regulatory Organization. When a US Futures Commission Merchant (**FCM**) is a member of more than one self-regulatory organization (**SRO**), the SROs may decide among themselves which of them will be primarily responsible for enforcing minimum financial and sales practice requirements.

DT   Department of the Treasury

DTB   Deutsche Terminborse. German futures and options fully computerized exchange, opened in Frankfurt in 1990.

DTC   Depository Transfer Check

DTC   Depository Trust Company. Member of the Federal Reserve System owned by brokerage houses and the New York Stock Exchange, a centralized securities repository where stock and bond certificates are exchanged.

DTCC   Depository Trust and Clearing Corporation. Settles for the New York Stock Exchange and **NASDAQ**.

DTI   Department of Trade and Industry. UK government department responsible for promoting trade with other countries and overseeing UK business and finance.

DVP   delivery versus payment. Method whereby the transfer of one currency does not proceed unless the transfer of the other currency is simultaneously taking place.

DWR   drawer

DWT   dead weight tonne

DZD   Algeria, dinar (international currency symbol)

E

E	Swaziland emalangeni; sing. lilangeni (currency)
€	euro. *See* **EUR** and **euro**.
E$	Eurodollar. American dollar deposited in Europe.
£E	Egyptian pound divided into 100 piastres of 100 milliemes (currency)
EA	economic adviser
EA	*Ente Autonomo*. Autonomous Corporation. (Italy)
EA	enterprise allowance
EAB	European American Bank
EAC	East African Community. The East African Community was formally established in 1999 in Arusha, Tanzania. The treaty that was signed by Kenya, Tanzania, and Uganda, sets the course for the establishment in the future of a common market and political federation. Its predecessor had lasted from 1967 to 1977 but had collapsed for a number of reasons. The member countries are aiming to negotiate the framework of a customs union by 2003.
EADB	East African Development Bank. Established originally under the Treaty for East African Co-operation in 1967 with Kenya, Tanzania, and Uganda as signatories, a new Charter for the Bank (with the same signatories) came into force in 1980.Under the original treaty the bank was confined to the provision of financial and technical assistance for the promotion of industrial development in member states but with the new charter its remit was broadened to include involvement in agriculture, forestry, tourism, transport, and the development of infrastructures, with preference for projects which promote regional cooperation.
EAEC	East African Economic Community
EAF	Euro Access Frankfurt (Germany)
EAGGF	European Agricultural Guidance and Guarantee Fund. Fund established under the common agricultural policy of the European Union. (**EU**)
EAMTC	European Association of Management Training Centres
EAPN	European Anti-Poverty Network (EU)
EAR	effective annual rate (of interest)

EAS	East African shilling (currency)
EASD	European Association of Securities Dealers
EASDAQ	*see* **NASDAQ EUROPE**
EASY	expense-account spending money
EAT	earnings after tax
EAT	Employment Appeals Tribunal
EB	Ethiopian birr divided into 100 cents (currency)
EBA	ECU Banking Association (EU)
EBAN	European Business Angels Network (EU)
EBG	Electronic Banking Group, established by the **BCBS**
EBIAT	earnings before interest after taxes
EBIC	European Banks International Corporation
EBIC	European Business Information Centre
EBIT	earnings before interest and taxes
EBITA	Earnings before interest, taxes, and amortization
EBITDA	Earnings before interest, taxes, depreciation, and amortization
EBRD	European Bank for Reconstruction and Development. The Bank was inaugurated on 15 April 1991; following the signing of the treaty to establish the EBRD in May 1990.

In 1991 the initial emphasis was placed on programmes to support the creation and strengthening of infrastructure; privatization, reform of the financial sector, including development of capital markets, and privatization of commercial banks; the development of productive competitive private sectors of small and medium-sized enterprises in industry, agriculture, and services; restructuring industrial sectors to put them on a competitive basis; encouraging foreign investment; and cleaning up the environment.

It had 41 original members; the European Commission, the European Investment Bank, all the EEC countries and all the countries of Eastern Europe except Albania. Albania became a member in October 1991, as did all the republics of the former USSR in March 1992. Membership was 62 in 2001.

Its founding capital was ecu 10m, of which the USA contributed 10 per cent, the UK, France, Germany, Italy, and Japan 8.5 per cent each, and the USSR 6 per cent. Capital in 2000 was ecu 20m. It was established to lend funds at market rates to central and eastern European companies and countries "which are committed to, and applying, the principles of multi-party democracy and market economics". Facilities were extended to the countries of the former USSR in 1992.

There is a Board of Governors with full management powers, and a 23-member Board of Directors which is involved in day-to-day operations.

EBS   Electronic Broking Service

EBT   earnings before taxes

EC   European Community, *see* **EU**

EC$ East Caribbean dollar divided into 100 cents (currency of Anguilla, Antigua and Barbuda, Dominica, Grenada, Montserrat, St Kitts and Nevis, St Lucia, and St Vincent and the Grenadines)

ECA   European Congress of Accountants

ECA   European Court of Auditors. Audits revenue and expenditure for **EU**.

ECAs   Export Credit Agencies. Agencies provide security to enable bank loans to be made available on behalf of overseas buyers.

ECB   European Central Bank. Institution that replaced the **EMI** on transition to the third stage of **EMU**, resulting in a single currency. The ECB is responsible for carrying out the monetary policy of the **EU**, with instructions coming from the decision-making bodies of the Executive Board and Governing Council. It supervises the **ESCB**, which conducts foreign-exchange operations, administers money in circulation, ensures the smooth operation of the payment systems, and manages the official reserves of member states. Known as Den Europæiske Centralbank (Denmark), Europese Centrale Bank (Netherlands), Europeiska Centralbanken (Sweden). *See also* **BCE**, **EKP**, **EKT**, and **EZB**.

ECBS   European Committee for Banking Standards

ECCB   Eastern Caribbean Central Bank. ECCB was established in 1983, replacing the East Caribbean Currency Authority (ECCA).

ECCI   European Confederation for Commerce and Industry

ECCOFEX   European Commission Coordinating Committee of Options and Futures Exchanges

ECE   Economic Commission for Europe (UN)

ECGB   Export Credit Guarantee Department. Established in 1919, a

UK government department for the provision of insurance cover against risks of default on export credit, and of cover against the risk of assets invested abroad being expropriated.

ECHO   Exchange Clearing House. UK clearing house for foreign exchange derivatives contracts.

ECHR   European Convention on Human Rights

ECIP   European Community Investment Partners. Programme which supports European investment and exports to Asia, Latin America, and the Mediterranean. In 1992-97 300 million **ECU** was devoted to this task. Aid is granted to four complementary areas: (i) the identification of projects and partners; (ii) operations prior to the formation of a joint venture; (iii) the financing of capital needs; and (iv) the provision of management training or assistance for joint ventures

ECLAC   Economic Commission for Latin America and the Caribbean

ECN   electronic communications network, a class of alternative trading systems (**ATS**)

ECO   Economic Co-operation Organization. An intergovernmental regional organization established in 1985 by Iran, Pakistan, and Turkey. ECO is the successor of the Regional Co-operation for Development (RCD) which was first established in 1964. ECO was later expanded in 1992 to include seven new members: Afghanistan, Azerbaijan, Kazakhstan, Kyrgyzstan, Tajikistan, Turkmenistan, and Uzbekistan. The objectives of the organization, stipulated in its Charter, the Treaty of Izmir, include the promotion of conditions for sustained economic growth in the region. While transport and communications, trade and investment, and energy are the high priority areas in ECO's scheme of work, other fields of cooperation such as industry, agriculture, health, science and education, drug control, and human development are also on the agenda.

e-COMMERCE
             trading goods and services over the Internet

ECOWAS   Economic Community of West African States. Founded in 1975 as a regional common market, and now aiming to operate a single currency zone by 2004, it later also became a political forum involved in the promotion of a democratic environment and the pursuit of fundamental human rights. In July 1993 it revised its treaty to assume responsibility for the regulation of regional armed conflicts, acknowledging the inextricable link between development and peace and security.

ECP	Eurocommercial paper. Short-term borrowing commercial paper (**CP**) issued in a Eurocurrency.
ECR	electronic cash register
ECR	European Commercial Register of companies (EU)
ECS	Ecuadorian sucre. Currency *now* replaced by the US$.
ECSC	European Coal and Steel Community. Treaty signed in Paris in 1951 providing for the pooling of coal and steel production by Belgium, France, the Federal Republic of Germany, Italy, Luxembourg, and the Netherlands, and regarded as the first step towards a united Europe. As a result two more communities came into being: the European Economic Community (**EEC**) and the European Atomic Energy Community (EAEC or EURATOM).
ECTA	European Communities Trademark Association
ECU	European currency unit. From 1 January 1999, replaced by the **euro**.
ED	estate duty
ED	ex dividend
ED	Exposure Draft for Statements of Standard Accounting Practice, *now* Financial Reporting Exposure Draft (**FRED**)
ED	extra dividend
E-Day	1 January 2002, the date of the final changeover to the **euro**
EDC	Economic Development Committee
EDF	European Development Fund. Fund established by the European Community in 1976 for the provision of aid finance to developing countries associated with the **EU** through the Lomé Convention, and also to certain non-associated states, and to a number of developing countries in the Mediterranean Basin
EDF	expected default frequency
EDGARS	Electronic Data Gathering, Analysis, and Retrieval System (US). Automated system for submission by companies who are required by law to file forms with the US Securities and Exchange Commission (**SEC**).
EDI	Economic Development Institute
EDI	electronic data interchange
EDIE	European Direct Investment in Europe (EU)
EDIT	Estate Duties Investment Trust (pronounced EDITH)
EDM	Executive Doctor of Management

EDP   electronic data processing

EDR   European Depository Receipt. EDR is a certificate representing ownership of the issuer's underlying shares. The EDR is denominated and quoted in **euro**s.

EDS   Electronic Data Services. Gives historical turnover information about securities traded on the London Stock Exchange (**LSE**).

EDSP   exchange delivery settlement price. Price for delivery or cast settlement of the instrument underlying a derivative traded in the London International Financial Futures and Options Exchange (**LIFFE**).

EEA   European Economic Area. Comprises the territory of **EFTA** and the **EU** after an agreement signed in 1992 and provides for the free movement of capital, goods, services, and workers. To ensure compliance with rules and regulations, EFTA countries agreed to accept over 80 per cent of the Community's rules pertaining to the single market. Nevertheless, the agreement does not include Switzerland, a situation caused by a "no" vote in a referendum. This delayed the ratification process and therefore meant that the EEA treaty did not come into force until 1 January 1994. But its significance was soon diminished by the entry into the **EU** of three **EFTA** countries on 1 January 1995 (Austria, Finland, and Sweden).

EEC   European Economic Community/Communities, *see* **EU**

EEF   Engineering Employers' Federation

EEIG   European Economic Interest Grouping

EEK   Estonia, kroon (international currency symbol)

EES   European Economic Space

EES   European Exchange System

EEZ   exclusive economic zone

EFAS   European Financial Analysts' Society

EFER   European Foundation for Entrepreneurship Research (EU)

EFEX   European Financial Expertise. Network to mobilize European public and private sector financial sector expertise for technical assistance programmes in Asian countries. (EU)

EFF   *effetto*. Bill/promissory note. (Italy)

EFF   Extended Fund Facility (**IMF**)

EFFAS   European Federation of Financial Analysts Societies (**EU**)

EFICON   electronic financial control

EFIFC	European Federation of Investment Funds and Companies
EFILWC	European Foundation for the Improvement of Living and Working Conditions (EU)
EFL	external financial limit
EFMA	European Financial Marketing Association
EFMD	European Foundation for Management Development (EU)
EFP	exchange for physicals. Transaction generally used by two hedgers who want to exchange futures for cash positions. Also referred to as Against Actuals or Versus Cash.
EFRAG	European Financial Reporting Advisory Group
EFT	electronic funds transfer. System for the transfer of funds automatically, by electronic means, from one account to another.
EFTA	European Free Trade Association. EFTA was formed in 1959 by Austria, Denmark, Norway, Portugal, Sweden, Switzerland, and the UK. Finland effectively joined in 1961 and Iceland in 1970. Denmark and the UK left in 1973, and Portugal in 1986 on joining the European Union (**EU**). EFTA and the EU reached agreement in 1992 for a European Economic Area (**EEA**) that included the member countries of both institutions. Provisions in the EEA agreement include free movements of products within the EEA from 1993 (special arrangements to cover food, energy, coal, and steel); EFTA to assume EU rules on company law, consumer protection, education, the environment, research and development, and social policy; EFTA to adopt EU competition rules on antitrust matters, abuse of a dominant position, public procurement, mergers and state aid.
EFTPOS	electronic funds transfer at point of sale
EFTS	electronic funds transfer system
EGLEI	European Group for Local Employment Initiatives (EU)
EGM	extraordinary general meeting. Shareholders' meeting called to discuss matters that cannot wait until the **AGM**.
EGP	Egypt, pound (international currency symbol)
EGR	earned growth rate
EI	endorsement irregular
EIA	economic impact assessment
EIB	European Investment Bank. International bank established in 1958 to provide loan finance for EU member countries and associated countries, for the purposes of regional

development, projects of common interest to the EU and projects for modernization and conversion.

EIB	Export-Import Bank
EIBUS	Export-Import Bank of the United States
EIBW	Export-Import Bank of Washington
EIC	earned income credit
EIC	European Investment Centre
EICF	European Investment Casters' Federation
EICP	European Index of Consumer Prices (EU)
EIP	equal instalments of principal
EIPA	European Insolvency Practitioners' Association (EU)
EIPG	Energy Investment Promotion Group (EU)
EIR	earned income relief
EIS	Enterprise Investment Scheme. Scheme promoting investment in unquoted companies by which qualifying gains are exempt from capital gains tax (**CGT**). (UK)
EITF	Emerging Issues Task Force. EITF was formed in 1984 in response to the recommendations of the **FASB**'s task force on timely financial reporting guidance and an FASB Invitation to Comment on those recommendations. Task Force members are drawn primarily from public accounting firms but also include representatives of large companies and major associations or preparers, such as the Financial Executives Institute and the Institute of Management Accountants. The chief accountant of the Securities and Exchange Commission attends Task Force meetings regularly as an observer with the privilege of the floor.
EKP	Euroopan Keskespankki. European Central Bank. (Finland)
EKR	Estonian kroon (currency)
EKT	Ευρωπαϊή Κεντρική Τράπεζα. European Central Bank. (Greece)
ELEC	European League for Economic Cooperation
ELLIPS	Electronic Large Value Interbank Payments (Belgium)
ELR	economic limit factor
ELS	electronic lodgement service. System for filing tax returns electronically. (UK)
ELS	Eurolink System (Germany)
ELs	eligible liabilities
EM	effective margin

EMA   European Monetary Agreement. Replaced by European Payments Union (**EPU**) in 1958.

EMBI   emerging markets bond index

EMCC   European Municipal Credit Community

EMCF   European Monetary Cooperation Fund. Pool of 20 per cent of each **EU** member's gold and dollar reserves, it acts as a credit facility.

EMCOF   European Monetary Cooperation Funding

EMH   efficient markets hypothesis

EMI   European Monetary Institute established under the Treaty on European Union. The forerunner of the European Central Bank. (**ECB**)

EMIFP   Euro-Mediterranean Facility and Partnership

EMIP   equivalent mean investment period

EMS   European Monetary System. Instituted by the then European Community in 1979 with two main purposes: (i) to stabilize the currencies of member states; and (ii) to create a joint reserve fund and ultimately a common monetary system, including a common currency.

EMTA   Emerging Markets Traders Association

EMTN   euro medium-term note

EMU   Economic and Monetary Union. The creation of an Economic and Monetary Union (EMU) in Europe was envisaged in the Maastricht treaty on European Union and began on 1 January 1999. Exchange rates between participating countries are fixed and a single interest rate will be set for all participants by a European Central Bank (**ECB**). The **euro** became a currency in its own right.

EMV   expected monetary value

EN   Euro norm. European standard.

e & o   errors and omissions

e & oe errors and omissions excepted

EOE   European Options Exchange. A market for traded options founded in Amsterdam in 1978. The market operates within the Amsterdam Stock Exchange.

EONIA   Euro Overnight Index Average

EOQ   economic order quantity

EPB   equivalent pension benefit

EPC   Economic Policy Committee (EU)

EPC	European political cooperation
EPCGS	Export Promotion Capital Goods Scheme
EPIC	Electronic Price Information Computer. London Stock Exchange system for recording and transmitting price *via* **TOPIC**.
EPN	Electronic Payments Network (US). A nationwide system that processes electronic payments on behalf of banks, savings and loan institutions, and credit unions. *Formerly* known as the Automated Clearing House.
EPO	European Patent Office. Established in 1973.
EPOS	electronic point of sale. System for recording sales using sophisticated cash tills which record the total amount to be paid by a customer, provide him or her with itemized bills, and simultaneously adjust the firm's stock records to assist the firm to plan its reordering of goods.
EPP	Estate protection policy
EPR	Earnings-Price Ratio (more commonly Price-Earnings Ratio, **PER**). General financial term for ratio of a share's market price to the company's earnings per share.
EPS	earnings per share
EPT	Excess Profits Tax
EPU	European Payments Union
ERA	Economic Regulatory Administration (US)
ERDF	European Regional Development Fund. Largest of the **EU**'s structural funds, it was established in 1975 to provide financial assistance to development infrastructure in regions showing particular need so as to reduce imbalances between regions of the EU.
ERGOM	European Research Group on Management
ERI	exchange rate index
ERISA	Employee Retirement Security Act. Act passed by the US Congress in 1974. It created the Pension Benefit Guarantee Corporation also known as **Penny Benny**.
ERM	Exchange Rate Mechanism. System of coordinating the currencies of European Union member states before full monetary union was established. Its aim was to maintain exchange rate stability. Central banks were not allowed to fluctuate their currencies more than a certain per cent above (ceiling rate) or below (minimum rate) a central rate established by comparing all the currencies in the **ERM** and the European Currency Unit, the **ECU**.

ERN	Eritrea, nakfa (international currency symbol)
ERNIC	earnings-related national insurance contribution (UK)
ERNIE	electronic random number indicator equipment. Premium bonds are a UK government security introduced in 1956 and prizes are drawn by ERNIE.
ERP	European Recovery Programme
ERP	extended redemption penalty
ERS	earnings related supplement
ERSA	Economic Research and Statistics Service
ERTA	Economic Recovery and Tax Act (1981). Federal legislation that enacted broad changes to reduce in general income tax liabilities for US tax payers.
ESAF	enhanced structural adjustment facility. Concessional facility, provided by the International Monetary Fund (**IMF**), for low-income member countries with protracted balance-of-payment problems; it makes available low-interest loans which support three-year programmes and carry an interest rate of 0.5 per cent, with a five-year grace period and a ten-year maturity.
ESAP	economic structural adjustment programme
ESAU	Economic and Statistics Analysis Unit. Established by the UK Department for International Development (**DFID**) aiming to improve the quality of donor and government strategies for poverty eradication.
ESC	Cape Verde escudo caboverdiano divided into 100 centavos (currency)
ESC	Portuguese escudo, *former* currency, *now* euro
ESC	European Social Charter. ESC was adopted by the European Council of the **EU** in 1989. The 12 rights contained in the ESC are: freedom of movement; employment and remuneration; social protection; improvement of living and working conditions; freedom of association and collective bargaining; worker information; consultation and participation; vocational training; equal treatment of men and women; health and safety protection at the workplace; pension rights; integration of those with disabilities; and protection of young people. Although not legally binding, the UK voted against it.
ESCB	European System of Central Banks. The ESCB is composed of the European Central Bank (**ECB**) and 15 National Central Banks (**NCB**s). The NCBs of the member states not participating in the **euro** area are members with special status; while they are allowed to conduct their respective national

monetary policies, they do not take part in decision making regarding the single monetary policy for the euro area and the implementation of these policies. The Governing Council of the ECB makes a distinction between the ESCB and the "Eurosystem" which is composed of the ECB and the 11 fully participating NCBs.

ESCS   Economics, Statistics and Cooperative Service

ESF   European Social Fund. Established in 1960, it is the main mechanism of EC/EU social policy providing financial assistance for retraining, job-creation schemes and vocational training. A high proportion of the funding (75 per cent) is targeted towards fighting youth unemployment. The Delors II budget package significantly increased the resources available to the ESF, while the focus was directed towards the reintegration of unemployed people into working life and the improvement of the functions of the labour market.

ESO   employee share ownership

ESOP   employee share ownership plan. Scheme whereby employees acquire shares in the company in which they are employed. In US known as employee stock option plan.

ESOP   employee stock option plan

ESOS   Executive Share Option Scheme

ESP   Spain, peseta (*former* currency, *now* euro), international currency symbol. *Also* currency of Andorra.

ESPRIT   European Strategic Programme for Research and Development in Information Technology (EU)

ESRI   Environment Systems Research Institute (UNEP)

ET   earnings threshold (UK, national insurance)

ETB   Ethiopia, birr (international currency symbol)

ETF   electronic transfer of funds

ETF   exchange-traded fund

ETUC   European Trade Union Confederation. Established in 1973, the ETUC is recognized by the EU, the Council of Europe, and **EFTA** as the only representative cross-sectoral trade union organization at a European level.

EU   European Union. Term used since November 1993 when the Maastricht Treaty entered into force. Earlier it was known as the European Community (**EC**) and before that as the European Economic Community (**EEC**).

EUI   European University Institute. Based in Florence, Italy.

EUR   euro. From 1 January 2002 the general currency of Austria, Belgium, Finland, France, Germany, Greece, Ireland, Italy, Luxembourg, Netherlands, Portugal, and Spain, replacing national currencies. *Also* currency of Andorra, Azores, French Guiana, Guadeloupe, Kosovo, Martinique, Mayotte, Monaco, Montenegro, Réunion, St Pierre et Miquelon, San Marino, and the Vatican (international currency symbol).

EUREX   Eureka Research Expert system. Established in 1985 on a French initiative for non-military industrial research in advanced technologies in Europe.

EUREX   European Options and Financial Futures Exchange, formed from the merger of the German and Swiss futures exchanges in 1998

EURIBOR Euro Interbank Offered Rate

Euro   EU currency from 1 January 1999 which replaced the **ECU**. On 1 January 2002 coins and notes went into circulation in the 12 Euro-zone countries replacing national currencies. *See also* **EUR**.

Eurobond interest-bearing security issued across national borders, usually in a currency other than that of the issuer's home country

EuroCCP European Control Counterparty. A UK clearing house supporting **NASDAQ EUROPE**.

Euroclear a settlement system for **Eurobond**s established in 1968 by a group of banks. It has facilities for accounting and dividend collection, and provides a clearing service. In addition it can provide working capital for dealers.

Eurofinas European Federation of Finance House Associations (EU)

EUROGIRO
            Integrated electronic network for transferring payments across European frontiers

EUROMED Euro-Mediterranean Partnership. Established by the Conference of **EU** foreign ministers held in Barcelona in November 1995. It is a joint initiative by the 27 partners on both sides of the Mediterranean: the 15 member states of the EU plus Algeria, Cyprus, Egypt, Israel, Jordan, Lebanon, Malta, Morocco, Syria, Tunisia, Turkey, and the Palestinian territories.

EURO.NM Grouping of regulated markets dedicated to growth companies, formed in 1996. Member exchanges are the Brussels Stock Exchange (Euro.NM Belgium), the Paris Stock Exchange (Le Nouveau Marché), the Deutsche Börse (Neue Markt), and the Amsterdam Stock Exchanges (NMAX).

EUROSTAT
Statistical support service for the EU based in Luxembourg. EUROSTAT collects statistics from each member state government and presents them in a consolidated, harmonized format.

EURO STOXX
index of leading European company shares

EV   expected value

EVA   economic value added. Method of evaluating companies by comparing the rate of return on investment with the weighted average cost of capital.

EVCA   European Venture Capital Association (EU)

EVR   electronic version of the tax return

EWI   Export Witness Institute

ex-   without. Prefix used to exclude certain benefits when shares are quoted.

EX B   ex bonus. Without bonus.

EX CAP   ex capitalization. Without capitalization.

EXCHEQ   exchequer

EX CP   ex coupon. Without the interest on the coupon.

EX DIV   ex divided. Excluding next dividend.

ex grat   *ex gratia*. Out of kindness. Payment given as a favour where no legal obligation exists.

Eximbank   Export-Import Bank. US bank founded in 1934 providing loans direct to foreign importers of US goods and services.

EX INT   ex interest. Without interest. *Also* EX In.

EX N   excluding new issue of shares

ex off   *ex officio*. By right of office.

EXOR   executor

E & Y   Ernst and Young LLP

EZB   Europäische Zentralbank. European Central Bank.

EZU   Europäische Zahlungsunion. European Payments Union.

91

F

F	finance
F	Dutch florin, *former* currency, *now* euro
F	French franc, *former* currency, *now* euro
F$	Fiji dollar divided into 100 cents (currency)
FA	*factura*. Invoice. (Spain)
FA	family allowance
FA	Finance Act
FA	financial adviser
FA	*Firma*. Firm/business. (Germany)
F & A	Finance and Accounting
FAA	free of all average. Insurance term meaning that total losses only will be paid.
FAAI	Fellow of the Institute of Administrative Accountants. No longer a valid qualification. The body is now the Institute of Financial Accountants (IFA) and their qualification is **FFA**.
FAAO	Finance and Accounts Office (US Army)
FABRP	Fellow of the Association of Business Recovery Professionals
FAC	finance administrative control
FAC	Food Aid Committee. Body established in the 1950s but since 1986 administering the Food Aid Convention forming part of the International Wheat Agreement (IWA). The task of the Food Aid Committee is to ensure the annual supply to developing countries of at least 7.5m tonnes of grain or grain products promised by each of the member governments of the Food Aid Convention. There are 23 member governments, all of them, with the exception of Argentina, industrialized countries. The actual target is 10m tonnes, and this has normally been exceeded.
FAC	Food Aid Convention. Established in 1967.
FACB	Fellow of the Association of Certified Book-keepers
FACCA	Fellow of the Association of Certified and Corporate Accountants (*now* the Chartered Association of Certified Accounts; *see* **FCCA**)

FACE	Financial Advertising Code of Ethics (US)
FACS	financial accounting and control system
FACS	floating-decimal abstract coding system
FACT	Federation Against Copyright Theft
FACTA	*factura*. Invoice. (Spain)
FACTS	financial accounting and control techniques for supply
FAE	final admitting examination
FAE	Foundation for Accounting Education
FAECC	Fellow of the Accountants and Executives Corporation of Canada
FAF	Financial Accounting Foundation. Established in 1972, the FAF is an independent, private-sector organization whose trustees are responsible for overseeing, funding and appointing members of the Financial Accounting Standards Board (**FASB**), the Government Accounting Standards Board (**GASB**) and their Advisory Councils. (US)
FAFC	Fellow of the Association of Financial Controllers and Administrators
FAG	Finance and Accounting Group (US)
FAI	free of all risks insurance
FAIA	Fellow of the Association of International Accountants
FAII	Fellow of the Australian Insurance Institute
FAL	funds at Lloyd's. Funds held in trust at Lloyd's to support a member's underwriting activities comprising their Lloyd's deposit, their personal reserve and their special reserve.
FAMIS	Financial and Management Information System
Fannie Mae	*see* **FNMA**
FAO	Finance and Accounts Office(r)
FAO	Food and Agriculture Organization of the United Nations. The FAO was founded in 1945 in Québec City. Its aims are to raise levels of nutrition and standards of living; to improve the production and distribution of all food and agricultural products from farms, forests and fisheries; to improve the living conditions of rural populations, and, by these means, to eliminate hunger. Its priority objectives are to encourage sustainable agriculture and rural development as part of a long-term strategy for the conservation and management of natural resources; and to ensure the availability of adequate food supplies, by maximizing stability in the flow of supplies and securing access to food by the poor.

F & AO	Finance and Accounts Office (US)
FAPA	Fellow of the Association of Authorised Public Accountants
FAQ	fair average quality
FAQ	free along quay
FAR	free asset ratio
FAS	financial accounting standards
FAS	free alongside ship
FASA	Fellow of the Australian Society of Accountants
FASA	First Auditor of Sheriff's Accounts (US)
FASAB	Federal Accounting Standards Advisory Board. Group authorized by the US accounting profession to establish generally accepted accounting principles (**GAAP**) applicable to federal government entities.
FASAC	Financial Accounting Standards Advisory Council
FASB	Financial Accounting Standards Board. Non-governmental body that sets the accounting rules for US companies. Although formal responsibility for rule-setting lies with the Securities and Exchange Commission (**SEC**), the latter leaves the task in the hands of the FASB, rarely intervening. FASB acts to improve the usefulness of financial reporting by focusing on the primary characteristics of relevance and reliability and on the qualities of comparability and consistency; keep standards current to reflect changes in methods of doing business and changes in the economic environment; consider promptly any significant areas of deficiency in financial reporting that might be improved through the standard-setting process; promote the international comparability of accounting standards concurrent with improving the quality of financial reporting, and improve the common understanding of the nature and purposes of information contained in financial reports.
FASBS	Statements of the Financial Accounting Standards Board
FATF	Financial Action Task Force. The world's main anti-money-laundering body. (**OECD**)
FBAA	Fellow of the British Association of Accountants and Auditors
FBIA	Fellow of the Bankers' Institute of Australia
FBIBA	Fellow of the British Insurance Brokers' Association
FBIM	Fellow of the British Institute of Management
FBINZ	Fellow of the Bankers' Institute of New Zealand

FBS	Fellow of the Building Societies Institute
FBT	fringe benefits tax. Any US federal income tax paid on an employee benefit received outside of salary but classified by the **IRS** as taxable income to the employee.
FBY	future budget year
FC	fixed charge
FCA	Fellow of the Institute of Chartered Accountants in England and Wales (also Fellow of the Institute of Chartered Accountants in Ireland)
FCAA	Fellow of the Australasian Institute of Cost Accountants
FCA(AUST)	Fellow of the Institute of Chartered Accountants in Australia
FCAI	Fellow of the New Zealand Institute of Cost Accountants
FCAS	Fellow of the Casualty Actuarial Society (US)
FCB	Fellow of the British Association of Communicators in Business
FCB	Foundation for Commercial Banks
FCBA	Fellow of the Canadian Bankers' Association
FCBI	Fellow of the Institute of Bookkeepers
FCC	Farm Credit Corporation (Canada)
FCCA	Fellow of the Association of Chartered Certified Accountants
FCCS	Fellow of the Corporation of Secretaries
FCDU	foreign currency deposit unit
FCE	Foreign Currency Exchange
FCEA	Fellow of the Institute of Cost and Executive Accountants
FCI	Fellow of the Institute of Commerce
FCI	Finance Corporation for Industry
FCIA	Fellow of the Canadian Institute of Actuaries
FCIA	Fellow of the Corporation of Insurance Agents
FCIA	Foreign Credit Insurance Association. Established in 1962 in the US by some four dozen insurance companies to underwrite the risk on default on export credit, particularly that refinanced by the Export-Import Bank with which it is closely associated.
FCIArb	Fellow of the Chartered Institute of Arbitrators
FCIB	Fellow of the Chartered Institute of Bankers
FCIB	Fellow of the Corporation of Insurance Brokers

FCIBS	Fellow of the Chartered Institute of Bankers in Scotland
FCII	Fellow of the Chartered Insurance Institute
FCIM	Fellow of the Chartered Institute of Marketing
FCIPD	Fellow of the Chartered Institute of Personnel and Development. Fellowship is available to members who can demonstrate 10 years' relevant experience at management level and appropriate continuing professional development.
FCIPS	Fellow of the Chartered Institute of Purchasing and Supply
FCIS	Fellow of the Institute of Chartered Secretaries and Administrators
FCM	Futures Commission Merchant. US individual or organization which solicits or accepts orders to buy or sell futures contracts or commodity options and accepts money or other assets from customers in connection with such orders.
FCMA	Fellow of the Chartered Institute of Management Accountants
FCMA	Fellow of the Institute of Cost and Management Accountants, *formerly* **FCWA**
FCO	*franco*. Free of charge. (France)
FCPA	Fellow of the Association of Certified Public Accountants (international)
FCPA	Foreign Corrupt Practices Act (US)
FCPE	former centrally planned economies
FCPWA	Fellow of the Faculty of Community, Personal, and Welfare Accounting
FCSFAC	Farm Credit System Financial Assistance Corporation
FCT	Fellow of the Association of Corporate Treasurers
FCU	Federal Credit Union(s)
FCUS	Federal Credit Union System
FCWA	Fellow of the Institute of Cost and Works Accountants, *now* **FCMA**
FD	Finance Department
F & D	freight and demurrage (insurance)
FDI	Foreign Direct Investment
FDIC	Federal Deposit Insurance Corporation. Independent agency that provides insurance coverage for deposits in both bank (through the Bank Insurance Fund) and savings institutions (through the Savings Association Insurance Fund) and con-

ducts periodic examinations of state-chartered banks that are not members of the US Federal Reserve System. Federally chartered banks are insured by FDIC for deposits up to a maximum of US$100,000.

FDI index   Foreign Direct Investment index. The United Nations Conference on Trade and Development (**UNCTAD**) created the index to highlight states that are particularly appealing to foreign investors. The FDI index measures foreign direct investment relative to the country's share of global GDP, employment and exports.

FDIT   Federal Daily Income Trust

FDP   foreign duty payable

FDP   funded delivery period

FEAMIS   Foreign Exchange Accounting and Management Information System

FEB   Fair Employment Board (US)

FEB   Financial and Economic Board

FECB   Foreign Exchange Control Board

FECDBA   Foreign Exchange and Currency Deposit Brokers' Association. Professional body for brokers dealing in foreign exchange and foreign currency deposits.

FED   Federal Reserve Board. US committee which runs the central bank in the USA.

FED   Federal Reserve System (US)

FED FUNDS
          Federal Funds (US)

FEE   Fédération des Experts Comptables Européens. European organization which includes all national accounting organizations.

FEER   fundamental equilibrium exchange rate

FEI   Financial Executive Institute (US)

FEOGA   Fond Européen d'Orientation et de Garantie Agriculturale. European Union's farm fund.

FEP   Financial Evaluation Program

FEPC   Fair Employment Practices Committee (US)

FEPI   final expenditure price index

FERF   Financial Executives Research Foundation

FESCO   Forum of European Securities Exchange Commissions, *now* **CESR**

FESE	Federation of European Securities Exchanges
FET	Federal Estate Tax (US)
FET	Federal Excise Tax (US). Taxes on certain consumer items, such as alcohol, tobacco, gasoline, firearms, and airline tickets.
FETCL	Foreign Exchange and Trade Central Law. Legislation, introduced in 1949, setting a standard form of settlement of import invoices. The settlement must conform to the Japanese national interest, and if this requirement is satisfied an import licence is issued. In other cases a special permit must be obtained from the Ministry of International Trade and Industry (**MITI**). Modifications were made in the law following Japan's entry to the Organization for Economic Co-operation and Development (**OECD**) and acceptance of that body's code of liberalization.
FFA	Fellow of the Faculty of Actuaries (Scotland)
FFA	Fellow of the Institute of Financial Accountants
FFB	Federal Financing Bank. US government-owned bank that consolidates financing activities of various government agencies to reduce borrowing costs.
FFC	Foreign Funds Control
FFCB	Federal Farm Credit Board
FFI	Fellow of the Faculty of Insurance
FFI	Finance for Industry, investment group subsequently renamed as Investors in Industry (UK)
FFLA	Federal Farm Loan Association
FFMC	Federal Farm Mortgage Corporation
FFO	funds from operations
F & FP	Force and Financial Program
FFPA	free from particular average
FFS	family financial statement
FGA	free of general average (insurance)
FGAA	Federal Government Accountants Association
FGT	Federal Gift Tax. Area of the US federal tax code concerned with taxpayers' gifts to others and the tax benefits and liabilities thereby created.
FHA	Federal Housing Administration. Its sole function is to encourage residential housing by providing mortgage insurance to builders and buyers of homes as well as to mortgage lenders. (US)

FHA	Finance Houses Association
FHFB	Federal Housing Finance Board. US government agency that oversees the Federal Home Loan Bank System, which replaced the Federal Home Loan Bank Board.
FHLB	Federal Home Loan Bank
FHLBB	Federal Home Loan Bank Board. US regulatory body for the savings and loan associations established in the 1930s. The Federal Home Loan Bank System provides credit reserve for mortgage lending institutions through 12 regional Home Loan banks. *Now* **OTS**.
FHLMC	Federal Home Loan Mortgage Corporation. Commonly called **Freddie Mac**, FHLMC also refers to mortgage-backed securities packaged, guaranteed, and sold by the organization. (US)
FIA	Federal Insurance Administration (US)
FIA	Fellow of the Institute of Actuaries
FIA	financial inventory accounting
FIA	Futures Industry Association. Trade Association for Futures Commission Merchants. (US)
FIAB	Fellow of the International Association of Book-keepers
FIAI	Fellow of the Institute of Industrial and Commercial Accountants
FIAII	Fellow of the Incorporated Australian Insurance Institute
FIANZ	Fellow of the Institute of Actuaries of New Zealand
FIB	Fellow of the Institute of Bankers
FIBA	Fellow of the Institute of Business Administration (Australia)
FIBOR	Frankfurt Inter-Bank Offered Rate
FIBScot	Fellow of the Institute of Bankers in Scotland
FIBV	Fédération Internationale des Bourses de Valeurs. International Federation of Stock Exchanges formed in 1961.
FICA	Federal Insurance Contributions Act. US federal legislation that provides retirement income and health benefits to the elderly, disabled, and other qualifying individuals and families. Also known as Social Security.
FICAI	Fellow of the Institute of Chartered Accountants in Ireland
FICB	Fellow of the Institute of Certified Book-keepers
FICBs	Federal Intermediate Credit Banks
FICEA	Fellow of the Association of Industrial and Commercial Executive Accountants

FICM   Fellow of the Institute of Credit Management

FICMA   Fellow of the Institute of Cost and Management Accountants

FICO   Financing Corporation

FID   foreign income dividend

FIEx   Fellow of the Institute of Export

FIF   First Investment Fund

FIFO   first in first out

FIFP   Fellow of the Institute of Financial Planning

FII   foreign institutional investors

FII   franked investment income

FII   Futures Investment Institute (US)

FIIA   Fellow of the Institute of Internal Auditors

FIIA   Financial Institution Insurance Association (US)

FIIT   Federal Individual Income Tax

FIL   Foreign Investment Law. Law regulating foreign investment in Japan between 1950 and 1979.

FIM   Finland, markka (*former* currency, *now* euro), international currency symbol

FIMBRA Financial Intermediaries, Managers, and Brokers Regulatory Association. Self regulatory body which was responsible for regulating firms which advise and act on behalf of members of the general public in financial dealings such as life assurance policies, unit trusts, etc. Its responsibilities are now controlled by the Financial Services Authority (**FSA**).

FIMC   Fellow of the Institute of Management Consultants

FIMgt   Fellow of the Institute of Management

FIMTA   Fellow of the Institute of Municipal Treasurers and Accountants

FIN   finance

FIN   financial

FIN   financier

FINEX   Financial Instrument Exchange

FInstAM Fellow of the Institute of Administrative Management

FInstSMM Fellow of the Institute of Sales and Marketing Management

FIPA   Fellow of the Insolvency Practitioners Association

FIR   financial inventory report

FIRA	Federal Investment Review Agency
FIRA	Foreign Investment Review Agency
FIRMA	Fiduciary and Investment Risk Management Association
FIRREA	Financial Institutions Reconstruction, Recovery and Enforcement Act. US federal tax legislation enacted in 1989 to resolve the crisis in the savings and loan industry.
FIRST	Financial Information Reporting System
FIS	family income supplement
FISC	Financial Industries Service Corporation
FISH	Finance Industry Standards Association
FISMA	Financial Services and Markets Act 2000
FIT	Federal Income Tax. Broad area of federal tax code concerned with tax obligations, owed on all types of income (US)
FIT	finance for innovative technology (EU)
FIT	free of income tax
FITW	federal income tax withholding (US)
FJD	Fiji, dollar (international currency symbol)
FKP	Falkland Islands, pound (international currency symbol)
Fkr	Faroese krone (currency)
FL	florin
FLA	Federal Loan Administration
FLA	Federal Loan Agency
FLA	Finance & Leasing Association
FLB	Federal Land Bank
FLBAs	Federal Land Bank Associations
FLIA (dip)	Fellow of the Life Insurance Association (Diploma)
FLR	fixed loan rate. Accounting and banking term for fixed lending rate as opposed to variable rate over the life of a loan.
FLRA	Federal Labor Relations Authority (US)
FLSA	Fair Labor Standards Act (US)
FMAAT	Fellow Member of the Association of Accounting Technicians
FMAI	Financial Management for Administrators Institute
FMCG	fast moving consumer goods
FMG	franc malgache divided into 100 centimes (Madagascan currency)

FmHA	Farmers Home Administration
FMI	Fondo Monetario Internacional. International Monetary Fund. (Spain)
FMI	Fonds Monétaire International. International Monetary Fund. (France)
FMK	Finnish markka, *former* currency, *now* euro
FMPEC	Financial Management Plan for Emergency Conditions (US)
FMS	Fellow of the Institute of Management Services
FMS	Financial Management System
FMS	flexible manufacturing system. Means of production that makes extensive use of programmed automation and computers to achieve rapid production of small batches of components or products while maintaining flexibility in manufacturing a wide range of these items.
FNB	First National Bank
FNBC	First National Bank of Chicago
FNCB	First National City Bank (US)
FNMA	Federal National Mortgage Association. US mortgage agency commonly called **Fannie Mae**.
FNSA	Fédération National des Sociétés d'Assurance. French national association of insurance companies.
FNSAGA	Fédération National des Syndicats d'Agents Généraux d'Assurance. French national association of independent general insurance sales agents.
FNV	Financiera Nacional de la Vivienda (National Housing Finance)
FNZSA	Fellow of the New Zealand Society of Accountants
FO	Finance Officer
FOB	free on board
FOC	free of charge
FOC	free of claims
FOCIS	Financial On-Line Central Information System
FOCUS	Financial and Operational Combined Uniform Single
FOEX	Finnish Options Exchange. Exchange trades in currency derivatives, Finnish government bonds, interest-rate options, and futures based on the wood-pulp price index (**PIX**).
FOF	futures and options fund
FoFs	funds of funds

FOG   flow of gold

FOIA   Freedom of Information Act (US)

FOK   fill or kill. Used on Stock Exchange as an order to carry out or cancel.

FOMC   Federal Open-Market Committee. Division of the Federal Reserve Bank responsible for setting interest rates and credit policies for the Federal Reserve System. Economists and market analysts watch the Committee's decisions closely as a means of predicting action by the Fed to stimulate the economy by tightening or loosening credit.

Footsie   *see* **FTSE 100 Index**

FOR   Hungarian forint (currency)

FOREX   foreign exchange

FOS   Financial Ombudsman Service. In 2001, the Financial Ombudsman Service became the single ombudsman for consumer complaints about financial products and services. It replaced the Banking and Building Societies Ombudsmen; the Insurance and Investment Ombudsmen; and the Securities and Futures Authority (**SFA**) Complaints Bureau. The Financial Ombudsman Service helps to resolve disputes where the consumer has already complained to a financial firm and remains dissatisfied. The firm the complaint is made about could be a bank, building society, insurance company, investment firm, financial adviser, unit trust company, or stockbroker. (UK)

FOT   free of tax

FOUSA   Finance Office(r), US Army

FOX   Futures and Options Exchange. **London FOX** became part of **LIFFE** in 1996.

FP   fully paid (of shares)

FPA   Financial Planning Association. Membership organization for the financial planning community, created when the Institute of Certified Financial Planners (**ICFP**) and the International Association for Financial Planning (**IAFP**) unified in 2000. Members include individuals and companies who have contributed to building the financial planning profession and all those who champion the financial planning process.

FPA   free of particular average (insurance)

FPC   Financial Planning Certificate

FPHA   Federal Public Housing Authority (US)

FPIF	fixed-price-incentive firm
FPMI	Fellow of the Pensions Management Institute
FPO	fixed price open
FPT	fixed price tender
FR	Federal Reserve (System)
FRA	forward rate agreement. Agreement whereby a currency is bought and sold at a future date at an agreed exchange rate.
FRANZ	Fellow Registered Accountant. Member of the New Zealand Society of Accountants.
FRB	Federal Reserve Board. The US Federal Reserve Board consists of seven governors appointed by Congress on the nomination of the President. They serve for 14 years. They establish Federal Reserve System policies on reserve requirements and other bank regulations, setting the discount rate, controlling the availability of credit in the country, and regulating the purchase of securities on margin.
FRBs	Federal Reserve Banks
FRC	Financial Reporting Council (UK)
FRCD	floating rate certificate of deposit. Certificate of deposit (**CD**) on which the issuing bank pays a variable coupon or interest rate.
FRED	Financial Reporting Exposure Draft (UK)
Freddie Mac	
	see **FHLMC**
FREF	Fixed Rate Export Finance
FRELP	Flexible Real Estate Loan Plan
FRF	France, franc. *Former* French currency, and the *former* currency of French Guiana, Guadeloupe, Martinique, Monaco, Réunion, and St Pierre et Miquelon (international currency symbol). *Now* euro.
FRI	Fellow of the Real Estate Institute
FRICS	Fellow of the Royal Institution of Chartered Surveyors
FRN	Federal Reserve Note
FRN	floating rate note. Euromarket note, the coupon of which alters according to interest rate changes.
FRRP	Financial Reporting Review Panel (UK)
FRS	Federal Reserve System. Central banking authority of the USA. It acts as the fiscal agent for the US government, is custodian of the reserve accounts of the commercial banks, and is authorized to issue the Federal Reserve notes that constitute the entire supply of paper currency of the country.

The System established under the Federal Reserve Act of 1913 comprises a Board of seven governors, the 12 regional Federal Reserve Banks and their 25 branches and the Federal Open-Market Committee (**FOMC**).

FRS   Financial Relations Society

FRSs   Financial Reporting Standards. Series of standards issued by the Accounting Standards Board (**ASB**) (UK). *See* Appendix 2.

FRSSE   financial reporting standard for smaller entities

FRU   Federal Reserve Unit

FS   financial statement

FSA   Federation of Schools of Accountancy

FSA   Finance Service – Army

FSA   Financial Services Act

FSA   Financial Services Authority. FSA became the UK's single statutory regulator for financial services on 30 November 2001. Its objectives are to maintain market confidence, promote public understanding of the financial system, protect consumers and fight financial crime.

FSA   foreign service allowance

FSA   forward spread agreement

FSAA   Fellow of the Society of Incorporated Accountants and Auditors, *now* amalgamated with Chartered Accountants

FSAVCs   freestanding addition voluntary contributions. Additional contributions to a pension scheme which is not part of the employer's scheme.

FSB   Federation of Small Businesses

FSBI   Fellow of the Savings Bank Institute

FSBR   Financial Statement and Budget Report. Document published by the Chancellor of the Exchequer (UK) on budget day. Also known as the Red Book.

FSC   Foreign Sales Corporation. Established by the Tax Reform Act of 1984. The FSC is a foreign corporation that exports for a US firm. The firm may show its profits in the FSC and avoid US taxation on a percentage of the earnings until they are remitted to the parent US firm.

FSC   Foreign Service Credits

FSCA   Fellow of the Institute of Company Accountants, *formerly* Fellow of the Society of Company and Commercial Accountants, but earlier designatory letters retained.

FSCA

FSCA   Fellow of the Society of Company and Commercial Accountants

FSCS   Financial Services Compensation Scheme (UK)

FSE   Federation of Stock Exchanges

FSFA   Fellow of the Society of Financial Advisers

FSIC   Federal Savings Insurance Corporation

FSLA   Federal Savings and Loan Association

FSLAC   Federal Savings and Loan Advisory Council

FSLIC   Federal Savings and Loan Insurance Corporation. US insurance company for savings and loan institutions and their depositors, *replaced* by Office of Thrift Supervision (**OTS**).

FT   *Financial Times*. Leading British financial daily newspaper. Printed on pink paper.

F & T   fire and theft (insurance)

FTA   Free Trade Agreement. Agreement signed between the USA and Canada in 1988 and ratified in 1989, abolishing all tariffs between the two countries.

FTA Index   *Financial Times* Actuaries Index

FTASI   *Financial Times* Actuaries All-Share Index

FTC   Federal Trade Commission. US government agency charged with investigating and enjoining illegal practices in interstate trade.

FTD   Federal tax deposit

FTE   full time equivalent

FTI   federal tax included

FTII   Fellow of the Chartered Institute of Taxation

FTII   Fellow of the Taxation Institute Incorporated

FTIT   Fellow of the Institute of Taxation

FTO   *Financial Times* (Industrial) Ordinary Share Index

FTSE   Actuaries All-Share Index. *Financial Times* Stock Exchange index designed to show the movement in market value of all UK companies listed on the London Stock Exchange.

FTSE 100 Index
  Financial Times Stock Exchange index of the largest 100 companies listed on the London Stock Exchange, often called the **Footsie**. It was introduced in January 1984 and provides a minute by minute indication of how the market is moving.

FT-SE   *see* **FTSE 100 Index**

106

FTT	Federal Transfer Tax. Large area of the federal tax code that comprises three tax regimes; federal estate tax (**FET**); federal gift tax (**FGT**); and the generation-skipping tax (GST).
FTZ	free-trade zone
FURBS	funded unapproved retirement benefit schemes. Top-up pension schemes for directors and other high earners whose salaries exceed the maximum level at which the UK government is prepared to give tax relief on contributions into a pension scheme. Because FURBS are "unapproved", they do not receive preferential tax treatment. Most are trust funds set up by employers or insurance policies to pay benefits to members in retirement.
FUT	futures
FUTA	Federal Unemployment Tax Act. US federal and state legislation that requires employers to contribute to a fund that pays unemployment insurance benefits for employees.
FUTOP	Guarantee Fund for Danish Options and Futures. Established in 1988 and merged with the Copenhagen Stock Exchange in 1997.
FV	future value. Value to which a sum of money will increase if invested for a certain period of time at a certain rate of interest.
FWA	Factories and Workshops Act
FWA	financial working arrangement
FX	foreign exchange
FXA	forward exchange agreement
FXnet	International system, set up in 1984, for the netting of bilateral foreign exchange trades between banks
FY	fiscal year (Canada, US)
FYA	first year allowance (taxation, UK)
FYP	five-year plan

G

G	gourde (Haitian currency)
G	grand (1000 dollars or pounds)
₲	guarani (Paraguayan currency)
G$	Guyana dollar (currency)
G3	Group of Three (most powerful industrial nations). They are USA, Germany, and Japan.
G5	Group of Five (nations that agreed to exchange rate stabilization). Five countries, France, Japan, UK, USA, and Germany, who agreed to stabilize their exchange rates by acting together to avoid adverse market forces. Also known as the Plaza Agreement, signed at the Plaza Hotel, New York in 1985.
G7	Group of Seven (major industrial nations). G7 was established in 1985 to discuss the world economy. The seven are: the USA, Canada, UK, France, Germany, Italy, and Japan. The grouping was later enlarged to include Russia and is now referred to as Group of Eight (**G8**).
G8	Group of Eight (major industrial nations). As Group of Seven (**G7**) with the addition of Russia.
G10	Examination paper on taxation and trusts for the Advanced Financial Planning Certificate (**AFPC**).
G10	Group of Ten, also known as the Paris Club. Nations lending money to the International Monetary Fund (**IMF**).
G20	Examination paper on personal financial planning for the Advanced Financial Planning Certificate (**AFPC**)
G24	Group of 24 (richest industrialized nations)
G30	Examination paper on business financial planning for the Advanced Financial Planning Certificate (**AFPC**)
G60	Examination paper on pensions for the Advanced Financial Planning Certificate (**AFPC**)
G70	Examination paper on portfolio management for the Advanced Financial Planning Certificate (**AFPC**)
G77	Group of 77 (developing countries). In fact there are more than 100 countries.

G80   Examination paper on long term care, life and health protection for the Advanced Financial Planning Certificate (**AFPC**)

GA   general average (insurance)

GA   government actuary

GAA   general accredited appraiser

GAAP   generally accepted accounting principles. Uniform minimum standards of and guidelines to financial accounting and reporting. At present, the Financial Accounting Standards Board (**FASB**), the Governmental Accounting Standards Board (**GASB**), the Federal Accounting Standards Advisory Board (**FASAB**), are authorized to establish these principles.

GAAR   general anti-avoidance rule (taxation)

GAAS   generally accepted auditing standards. Accounting term for body of knowledge for the proper conducting of accounting audits, promulgated by the American Institute of Certified Public Accounts (**AICPA**) and interpretations of which are issued in the form of Statements on Auditing Standards (**SAS**). The 10 fundamental standards are grouped as follows: general standards, standards of fieldwork, and reporting standards.

GAB   general arrangements to borrow (International Monetary Fund, **IMF**)

GACHA   Georgia Automated Clearing House Association (US)

G&AE   general and administrative expense(s)

GAFTA   Grain and Feed Trade Association. Controlling body of the London Grain Futures Market, a commodity market for wheat and barley that trades on the floor of the Baltic Exchange.

GAI   guaranteed annual income (US)

GAO   General Accounting Office. US government department, headed by the Comptroller General.

GAR   guaranteed annuity rate

GASAC   Governmental Accounting Standards Advisory Council

GASB   Governmental Accounting Standards Board. US government agency, organized in 1984, establishing accounting standards for both government and business.

GASBS   Statements of the Governmental Accounting Standards Board

GATT   General Agreement on Tariffs and Trade. International organization established in 1947 to promote the expansion of international trade through the removal of tariffs and other restrictions on cross-frontier trade. GATT operated in two principal ways: (i) by arranging for countries to receive foreign tariff reductions in return for tariff cuts of their own (reciprocity); (ii) by requiring that a country should apply its lowest tariff for any particular product to all of its suppliers (the "most favoured nation" rule).

In 1995 GATT was replaced by the World Trade Organization (**WTO**).

GAV   gross annual value

GBO   goods in bad order

GBP   Great Britain, pound sterling (international currency symbol)

GBR   government borrowing rate (UK)

GC   generalized collateral

GCC   Gulf Co-operation Council. Established in 1981 aiming to: assure security and stability of the region through economic and political cooperation; promote, expand, and enhance economic ties on solid foundations, in the best interests of the people; coordinate and unify economic, financial, and monetary policies, as well as commercial and industrial legislation and customs regulations; and achieve self-sufficiency in basic foodstuffs.

GCM   General Clearing Member of London Clearing House

GDDS   General Data Dissemination Standard (International Monetary Fund, **IMF**)

GDP   gross domestic product. Measures the money value, at market prices, of the goods and services produced by the economy in a period of time, usually a year.

GDR   global depositary receipt. Certificate that represents ownership of a given number of a company's shares and that can be listed or traded independently from the underlying assets.

GEF   Global Environment Facility. UN Environment Programme (**UNEP**) US$2000 million fund to help countries translate global concerns into national action so as to help fight ozone depletion, global warming, loss of biodiversity, and pollution of international waters.

GEL   Georgia, lari (international currency symbol)

GEMMs   Gilt-edged market makers

GEMU   German Economic and Monetary Union. Process of integrating economic and monetary conditions in former East and West Germany, following unification.

GES	*Gesellschaft.* Company or Society. (Germany)
GETT	grants equal to tax
GF	Guinean franc (currency)
GFCF	gross fixed capital formation
GFOFs	geared futures and options funds
GFTU	General Federation of Trade Unions (US)
GHC	Ghana, cedi (international currency symbol)
GIC	General Investment Corporation
GIC	Guaranteed Investment Contract/Certificate
GICS	Global Industry Classification Standard
Ginnie Mae	*see* **GNMA**
GIP	Gibraltar, pound (international currency symbol)
GISC	General Insurance Standards Council (UK)
GLB	Gramm-Leach-Bliley Act 1999. US banking law which became effective in March 2000. This Act repealed provisions of the Glass-Steagall Act that restricted affiliations between commercial and investment banks.
GLOBEX	Overnight electronic trading system developed in 1992 jointly by the Chicago Mercantile Exchange, the Chicago Board of Trade, and Reuters, dealing in currency futures and options
GM	general mortgage
GmbH	*Gesellschaft mit beschränkter Haftung.* German private limited company.
GMC	Guaranteed Mortgage Certificate
GMD	Gambia, dalasi (international currency symbol)
GMP	guaranteed minimum pension
GNMA	Government National Mortgage Association. Commonly called **Ginnie Mae**, a government-owned corporation that primarily issues securities that pass through all payments of interest and principal received on a pool of federally insured mortgage loans. GNMA guarantees that all payments of principal and interest will be made on the mortgages on a timely basis.
GNP	gross national product. Total money value of all goods and services produced in an economy over a one-year period (gross domestic product, **GDP**) plus property income from abroad (profits, dividends, rent, and interest).

111

GNS   guineas

GOFO   Gold Forward Offered Rate. Rate at which dealers will lend gold on swap against US dollars.

GOMA   general officer money allowance

GOOA   gilt-edged official operations account (UK)

GOU   gourde (Haitian currency)

GPM   graduated payment mortgage (US)

GPP schemes
             group personal pensions schemes

GPS   graduated pension scheme

GRD   Greece, drachma (*former* currency, *now* euro), international currency symbol

GRE   grant-related expenditure

GRI   Graduate, Realtor Institute

GRI   guaranteed retirement income (New Zealand)

GRID   Global Resource Information Database (**UNEP**)

GRN   goods received note

GRSP   General Revenue Sharing Programme

GRT   gross registered tonne

GS   gold standard, monetary unit in which the currency unit is a fixed weight of gold or its equivalent to the value of gold, on which there are no trading restrictions. Britain returned to the GS in 1925, a contributory factor in the economic depression, and finally left it in 1931.

GSB   Government Savings Bank

GSE   Government-sponsored enterprise (US)

GSL   guaranteed student loan (US)

GS & LA Guam Savings and Loan Association

GSP   Generalized System of Preference. System of preferential treatment given by the EU to non-member states such as those covered by the Yaoundé Convention.

GST   goods and services tax. Equivalent to **VAT** in New Zealand and Canada.

GTC   good till cancelled. Order for a commodity remaining open for execution so long as not specifically cancelled.

GTQ   Guatemala, quetzal (international currency symbol)

GULP   Group Universal Life Policy. Life assurance policy offered to employees and, sometimes, their family members, on a group basis, therefore less expensively than individuals could obtain personally.

GVA   gross value added

GWP   gross world product

GYD   Guyana, dollar divided into 100 cents (international currency symbol)

GZ   Girozentrale Vienna, Austrian Central Bank

H

H	*hacienda*. Treasury. (Spain)
H15	Examination paper on supervision and sales management for the Advanced Financial Planning Certificate (**AFPC**) qualification
H25	Examination paper on "holistic" financial planning for the Advanced Financial Planning Certificate (**AFPC**) qualification
HAT	Housing Association Trust
HBG	Hongkong Bank Group
HBS	Harvard Business School
HC	Hard Copy. Business management term for a physical paper document as opposed to an electronic document.
HC	held covered (insurance)
HCF	health care financing
HCFA	Health Care Financing Administration
HCPI	Harmonized Consumer Price Index (EU)
HDI	Human Development Index. Index produced by the UN Development Programme which is a broader measure of economic and social progress than **GDP** per head, and a more conventional gauge of living standards. The HDI combines three indicators of well-being: life expectancy, GDP per head, and educational attainment, including adult literacy and enrolment in schools and universities. In general, rich countries have higher rankings on this index than poorer ones.
HEC	*(école des) hautes études commerciales*. College of higher commercial studies. (France and Canada)
HERMES	Hellenic Real-time Money Transfer Express System (Greece)
HEX	Helsinki Stock Exchange share index
H/F	*Hlutafjelagid*. Limited company. (Iceland)
HFC	Household Finance Corporation
HFM	hold for money
HFMA	Health Care Financial Management Association
HICP	harmonized index of consumer prices
HIDB	Highlands and Islands Development Board
HIP	health insurance plan (US)

HIPC	highly indebted poor countries
HK	housekeeper allowance
HK$	Hong Kong dollar divided into 100 cents
HKD	Hong Kong, dollar (international currency symbol)
HKFE	Hong Kong Futures Exchange
HK & S	Hongkong and Shanghai Bank
HLBB	Home Loan Bank Board (US)
HMC	Household Mortgage Corporation
HMI	Her/His Majesty's Inspector
HMIT	Her/His Majesty's Inspector of Taxes
HMSO	Her/His Majesty's Stationery Office. *Now* the Stationery Office (**tSO**)
HMT	Her Majesty's Treasury
HNL	Honduras, lempira (international currency symbol)
HP	hire purchase. Method of financing the purchase of assets. Under an HP agreement the customer will pay an initial deposit, with the remainder of the balance and interest paid over a period of time. The assets can be used immediately while allowing repayments to be staggered, giving borrowers a better cash flow.
HPG	High Premiums Group. Group of Names investing substantially in Lloyd's of London and established to safeguard the interests of its members following a period of turbulence.
HPTA	Hire Purchase Trade Association
HRD	human resource development
HRK	Croatia, kuna (international currency symbol)
HRM	human resource management
HRP	home responsibilities protection (UK, pensions)
HSBC	Hongkong and Shanghai Banking Corporation
HSN	Harmonized System Nomenclature. *Formerly* Brussels Tariff Nomenclature (**BTN**) *and then* Customs Cooperation Council Nomenclature (**CCCN**).
HTG	Haiti, gourde (international currency symbol)
HUD	Department of Housing and Urban Development. US government agency responsible for stimulating and guiding the housing development industry.
HUF	Hungary, forint (international currency symbol)
HVB	HypoVereinbank. Second largest bank in Germany.

I

IA	incorporated accountant
IA	initial allowance
IA	Institute of Actuaries
IAA	Insurance Accounting Association
IAA	International Actuaries Association
IAB	Inter-American Bank
IAB	International Association of Book-keepers
IABLA	Inter-American Bank for Latin America
IACCP	Inter-American Council of Commerce and Production
IACP	International Association of Computer Programmers
IADB	Inter-American Development Bank
IAFP	International Association for Financial Planning
IAG	International Auditing Guidelines
IAHA	International Association of Hospitality Accountants
IAI	Independent Accountants International
IAPC	International Auditing Practices Committee
IAPS	International Auditing Practice Statement
IARB	Institute of Arbitrators
IARIW	International Association for Research into Income and Wealth
IAS	International Accountants Society
IAS	*International Accounting Standards*. Established by International Accounting Standards Committee (**IASC**) to attempt to standardize accounting practice internationally.
IASA	Insurance Accounting and Statistical Association
IASB	International Accounting Standards Board. US organization whose members represent 153 accounting bodies in 112 countries. The group is dedicated to bringing about the harmonization of international accounting standards.
IASC	International Accounting Standards Committee. Organization based in London aiming to reach global agreement on accounting standards. It publishes *International Accounting Standards*.
IASG	Inflation Accounting Steering Group

116

IASS	Insurance Accounting and Statistical Society
IB	Institute of Bankers
IB	International Bank (for Reconstruction and Development)
IB	introducing broker
IB	Istanbul Bankasi. Istanbul Bank. (Turkey)
IBA	Independent Bankers' Association
IBA	Indian Banks Association
IBA	Industrial Bankers' Association
IBA	industrial buildings allowance
IBA	Investment Bankers' Association
IBAA	Independent Bankers' Association of America
IBAA	Investment Bankers' Association of America
IBAN	International Bank Account Number
IBBR	interbank bid rate
IBD	interest-bearing deposit
IBEC	International Bank for Economic Cooperation
IBELs	interest-bearing eligible liabilities
IBEX-35	Principal Index of the Spanish stock exchanges
IBF	international banking facility
IBFD	International Bureau of Fiscal Documentation
IBI	Instituto Bancario Italiano. Italian Banking Institute.
IBIS	Interbank Information System
IBMBR	interbank market bid rate
IBNR	incurred but not reported (insurance)
IBOP	international balance of payments
IBOS	Inter-Bank On-Line System. A London-based currency payment management system.
IBRC	Insurance Brokers' Registration Council
IBRD	International Bank for Reconstruction and Development. IBRD came into being at the UN Monetary and Financial Conference at Bretton Woods (New Hampshire, USA) in July 1944. IBRD, frequently called the World Bank, began operations in 1946, its purpose being to provide funds, policy guidance, and technical assistance to facilitate economic development in its poorer member countries. *See* World Bank (**WB**). (UN)
IBRO	International Bank Research Organization

IB Scot   Institute of Bankers in Scotland

ICA   invalid care allowance (UK)

I of CA   Institute of Chartered Accountants

ICAA   integrated cost-accounting application(s)

ICAB   International Cargo Advisory Body

ICAEW   Institute of Chartered Accountants in England and Wales

ICAI   Institute of Chartered Accountants in Ireland

ICAR   International Center for Accountancy Reform (US)

ICAS   Institute of Chartered Accountants of Scotland

ICB   International City Bank

ICBC   International Commercial Bank of China

ICC   International Chamber of Commerce. World Federation founded in 1920, to promote international trade. Membership consists of business organizations, firms, and businessmen and women. Its objectives are to express, and to represent to governments, the considered judgements of international businesses on current problems of international trade, to improve trading conditions, and to foster private enterprise.

ICC   Interstate Commerce Commission (US)

IC & C   invoice cost and charges

ICCA   International Consumer Credit Association

ICCH   International Commodities Clearing House. Clearing house for futures dealings in the London commodity market. First began operating in 1888, as the London Produce Clearing House, becoming ICCH in 1973. It deals in most soft commodities (except wheat and barley) and most metals.

ICD   investment certificates of deposit

ICF   Industrial and Commercial Finance Corporation (now part of Investors in Industry)

ICFP   Institute for Certified Financial Planners

ICFTU   International Confederation of Free Trade Unions. ICFTU was founded in 1949 following the withdrawal of some Western trade unions from the World Federation of Trade Unions (**WFTU**), which had come under Communist control. The constitution, as amended, provides for cooperation with the **UN** and the **ILO**, and for regional organizations to promote free trade unionism, especially in developing countries. ICFTU aims to promote the interests of working people and to secure recognition of workers' organizations as free bargaining agents; to reduce the gap between rich and poor; and to defend fundamental human and trade union rights.

ICI	Investment Company Institute
ICIA	International Credit Insurance Association
ICM	Institute of Credit Management
ICM	intercostal margin
IComA	Institute of Company Accountants (UK). The Institute adopted its present title in September 1990. Before that date it was known as The Society of Company and Commercial Accountants – the name having been adopted in 1974 when three professional accounting bodies, all of long standing and with similar objectives, merged their membership to form the Society. The merging bodies were: The Institute of Company Accountants (established in Birmingham in 1928); The Incorporated Association of Cost and Industrial Accountants (Essex, 1937) and The Society of Commercial Accountants (Bristol, 1942). The present title is therefore that of one of the 1974 founding bodies. A further amalgamation in 1981 with another professional accountancy body, The British Association of Accountants and Auditors (Manchester, 1923), further enlarged the membership of the Institute fulfilling the specialist role of meeting the accountancy needs of smaller businesses. Members of the Institute use either the styling "Incorporated Company Accountant" or "Incorporated Practising Accountant". Fellows and Associates use respectively the designatory letters **FSCA** and **ASCA**.
ICPFs	insurance companies and pension funds
ICQ	internal control questionnaire
ICQ	invested capital questionnaire
ICS	instalment credit selling
ICS	Investors' Compensation Scheme
ICSA	Institute of Chartered Secretaries and Administrators
ICSID	International Center for the Settlement of Investment Disputes. Founded in 1966 to promote increased flows of international investment by providing facilities for the conciliation and arbitration of disputes between governments and foreign investors. It does not engage in such conciliation or arbitration. This is the task of conciliators and arbitrators appointed by the contracting parties. Recourse to conciliation and arbitration by members is entirely voluntary.
ICT	information and communication technology
ID	Iraqi dinar divided into 1,000 fils (currency)
IDA	International Development Association. The Association is a lending agency established in 1960 and administered by the

IBRD to provide assistance on concessional terms to the poorest developing countries. Its resources consist of subscriptions and general replenishments from its more industrialized and developed members, special contributions, and transfers from the net earnings of IBRD. *See* World Bank **(WB)**.

IDB   illicit diamond buyer/buying

IDB   Industrial Development Bank

IDB   Inter-American Development Bank. IDB, the oldest and largest regional multilateral development institution, was established in 1959 to help accelerate economic and social development in Latin America and the Caribbean.

IDB   inter-dealer broker

IDB   Islamic Development Bank. Agreement establishing the Islamic Development Bank (Banque islamique de développement) was adopted at the Second Islamic Finance Ministers' Conference held in Jeddah, Saudi Arabia, in August 1974. The Bank, which is open to all member countries of the Organization of the Islamic Conference, commenced operations in 1975. Its main objective is to foster economic development and social progress of member countries and Muslim communities individually as well as jointly in accordance with the principles of the Sharia.

IDBP   Industrial Development Bank of Pakistan

IDBT   Industrial Development Bank of Turkey

IDP   Institute of Data Processing

IDR   Indonesia, rupiah (international currency symbol)

IDR   International Depositary Receipt

IDS   Incomes Data Services

IEA   International Energy Agency. Autonomous agency within the Organization for Economic Cooperation and Development **(OECD)**; the IEA objectives include improvement of global energy cooperation, developing alternative energy sources, and the promotion of relations between oil-producing and oil-consuming countries.

IEB   International Energy Bank

IEP   Ireland (Eire), punt (*former* currency, *now* euro), international currency symbol

IET   interest equalization tax. US tax introduced in 1963, with the effect of raising the cost to US citizens of investing in issues by foreigners on the domestic US capital market.

IFA	independent fee appraiser
IFA	independent financial adviser
IFA	Institute of Financial Accountants
IFAA	Independent Financial Advisers Association (UK)
IFAC	International Federation of Accountants
IFAD	International Federation for Accountancy Development
IFAD	International Forum on Accountancy Development
IFAD	International Fund for Agricultural Development. IFAD's purpose is to mobilize additional funds for improved food production and better nutrition among low-income groups in developing countries, through projects and programmes directly benefiting the poorest rural populations while preserving their natural resource base.
IFB	invitation for bid
IFC	International Finance Corporation. Established in 1956, it is a member of the World Bank Group. It promotes private sector investment in developing countries which aims to reduce poverty and improve the quality of people's lives. It finances private sector projects that are profit-oriented, and environmentally and socially sound, and helps to foster development. IFC has a staff of 2000 professionals around the world who seek profitable and creative solutions to complex business issues. *See* World Bank (**WB**).
IFEBS	Integrated Foreign Exchange and Banking System
IFI	International Financial Institutions
IFMS	Integrated Financial Management System
IFNB	Idaho First National Bank
IFOX	Irish Futures and Options Exchange
IFP	Institute of Financial Planning (UK)
IFP	International Federation of Purchasing
IFRS	International Financial Reporting Standards
IFS	Institute for Fiscal Studies. Pressure group established in 1969 to conduct research in, and publish papers on, taxation and related issues. (UK)
IFS	Institute of Financial Services, official brand of the Chartered Institute of Bankers, providing courses and accreditation.
IFSL	International Financial Services, London. Successor organization to British Invisibles.
IGA	International Grains Agreement

IGC   Intergovernmental Conference. Conference of **EU** member governments called for the purpose of making changes in the Treaty of Rome. An IGC was convened for the adoption of the Maastricht Treaty and for its successor, the Amsterdam Treaty.

IGC   International Grains Council. Intergovernmental body helping governments in the implementation of the International Grains Agreement (**IGA**)

IGD   illicit gold dealer

IGE   *Imposta Generale sull'Entrata*. Turnover tax. (Italy)

IHT   Inheritance Tax. Tax levied on any transfer of assets to other people or trusts. It is most commonly paid in respect of an individual's estate on death, but it can also apply in respect of certain transfers of assets during life. IHT is often perceived as a voluntary tax; this is because with careful planning, it is possible to reduce or remove any liability altogether. If an individual dies when they are "domiciled" or "deemed domiciled" in the UK, then inheritance tax applies in respect of all their property, wherever situated. Domicile is a technical concept which identifies the permanent home of the taxpayer. If the deceased died domiciled abroad, then the tax only applies to property situated in the UK. It has been said that "Inheritance tax is, broadly speaking, a voluntary levy paid by those who distrust their heirs more than they dislike the Inland Revenue". (UK)

IIA   Institute of Internal Auditors

IIB   Institute of Insurance Brokers. Founded in 1987 as an association of independent insurance brokers. (UK)

IIB   International Investment Bank

IIB   Internordic Investment Bank

IIB   Iowa Independent Bankers' Association (US)

IID   Insurance Intermediate Directive

IIF   Institute of International Finance

IIMC   Institute for Investment Management Consultants

IIS   Internationales Institut der Sparkassen. International Institute of Savings Banks. (Germany)

I-J FC   Iselin-Jefferson Financial Company

ILC   irrevocable letter of credit

ILO   International Labour Organization. The Organization has been a specialized agency of the United Nations since 1946.

It was constituted in 1919 as an autonomous organization of the League of Nations. Its aim is to improve labour conditions through international action. Membership of the League carried with it membership of the Organization.

One of the ILO's principal functions is the formulation of international standards for living and working conditions, thereby encouraging social justice as a basis for securing world peace. Member countries are required to submit Conventions to their competent national authorities with a view to ratification. If a country ratifies a Convention it agrees to bring its laws into line with its terms and to report periodically on how these regulations are being applied.

ILS   index-linked note/security

ILS   Israel, shekel (international currency symbol)

ILU   Institute of London Underwriters. Founded in 1884.

IMA   Institute of Management Accountants

IMAMQ   Investment Management Asset Management Qualification

IMC   Institute of Management Consultancy

IMC   Investment Management Certificate, awarded by the Society of Investment Professionals (**SIP**). (UK)

IMCO   Inter-Governmental Maritime Consultative Organization. *Now* **IMO**.

IMF   International Monetary Fund. The IMF was established in 1945 and began financial operations in 1947. It aims to promote international monetary cooperation, to expand international trade and exchange rate stability; to assist in the removal of exchange restrictions and the establishment of a multilateral system of payments; and to alleviate any serious disequilibrium in members' international balance of payments by making the financial resources of the IMF available to them, usually subject to economic policy conditions to ensure the revolving nature of IMF resources.

IMFI   International Monetary Fund Institute

IMI   Instituto Mobiliare Italiano. Italian Assets Institution.

IMKB   Istanbul Menkul Kiymetter Borsasi. Share price index of the Istanbul Stock Exchange.

IMM   International Monetary Market

IMO   International Maritime Organization. IMO (*formerly* the InterGovernmental Maritime Consultative Organization, **IMCO**) was established as a specialized agency of the UN by a convention drafted in 1948 at a UN maritime conference in

Geneva. Its aims are to facilitate cooperation among governments on technical matters affecting merchant shipping, especially concerning safety at sea; to prevent and control marine pollution caused by ships; and to facilitate international maritime traffic.

IMRO — Investment Managers' Regulatory Organisation. Now regulated by the Financial Services Authority (**FSA**).

IMTA — Institute of Municipal Treasurers and Accountants

INBUCON — International Business Consultants

INC — incorporated. Form of registered company or other corporate body. (US)

INCFO — Institute of Newspaper Controllers and Finance Officers

INR — India, rupee (international currency symbol)

INRA — International Natural Rubber Agreement

INRO — International Natural Rubber Organization. Intergovernmental organization comprising six producer and 10 consumer members (the European Union being counted as one consumer country), based in Kuala Lumpur and formed to administer the International Natural Rubber Agreements.

INS — insurance

INSEAD — Institut Européen d'Administration des Affaires. European Institute of Administrative Affairs. (France)

INV — invoice

IO — interest-only strip

IOB — Institute of Bankers, *now* Chartered Institute of Bankers (**CIB**)

IOB — Institute of Book-keepers

IOB — Insurance Ombudsman Bureau

IOBI — Institute of Bankers in Ireland

IOBS — Institute of Bankers in Scotland

IOC order — immediate or cancelled order

IoD — Institute of Directors

IoE — Institute of Export

IOM — Index and Option Market. A division of the **CME**.

IoM — Institute of Management

IOS — Investors Overseas Services

IOSCo — International Organization of Securities Commissions. Association of leading stock market regulators formed in 1987.

IOU	I owe you. Signed document promising to repay money borrowed.
IP	information provider
IP	insolvency practitioner
IPA	individual pension account
IPA	Insolvency Practitioners Association
IPAI	International Primary Aluminium Institute. International association founded in 1972.
IP & BE	initial program and budget estimate
IPD	Institute of Personnel and Development
IPD	Investment Property Databank
IPE	International Petroleum Exchange. Commodity market for petroleum. (UK)
IPFA	Institute of Public Finance Accountants
IPO	Initial Public Offering. Offering of shares in the equity of a company to the public for the first time.
IPR	Individual Pay Record
IPS	inflation-protected securities
IPT	insurance premium tax. UK tax introduced in 1994 which applies to all general insurance premiums, including private medical insurance.
IQ	international quota
IQAB	International Qualifications Appraisal Board
IQD	Iraq, dinar (international currency symbol)
IR	Inland Revenue. UK government department responsible for the collection and administration of most taxes. Value added tax, excise tax and customs duties are the responsibility of HM Customs and Excise.
IR	Internal Revenue
IR	Iran, rial (currency)
IR£	Irish punt, divided into 100 pence, *former* currency, *now* euro
IRA	individual retirement account (US)
IRB	industrial revenue bond
IRC	Internal Revenue Code
IRF	International Road Federation. The IRF is a non-profit, non-political service organization whose purpose is to encourage better road and transportation systems worldwide and to

help apply technology and management practices to give maximum economic and social returns from national road investments. Founded following World War II, over the years the IRF has led major global road infrastructure developments, including achieving 1000 km of new road in Mexico in the 1950s, and promoting the Pan-American Highway linking North and South America.

IRFC   Ingersoll-Rand Finance Corporation

IRIS   Irish Real-time Interbank Settlement (Ireland)

IRO   interest rate options

IRO   Internal Revenue Office(r)

IRR   internal rate of return

IRR   Iran, rial (international currency symbol)

IRRV   Institute of Revenues, Rating, and Valuation

IRS   industrial relations services

IRS   interest rate swaps

IRS   Internal Revenue Service. US government agency that collects federal taxes and investigates tax illegalities. It also administers the US Department of Treasury regulations.

IRSF   Inland Revenue Staff Federation

Is£   Israeli pound (currency)

ISA   Individual Savings Account. The UK government introduced ISAs on 6 April 1999. On that date, ISAs replaced **PEP**s and **TESSA**s. No further investments are now allowed into the latter, although investors can retain existing investments within them tax-free. ISAs offer similar tax-free benefits to PEPs, but investors can hold a wider range of investments within ISAs, including stocks and shares, single-premium life assurance, and cash.

ISA   International Standard on Auditing

ISCC   International Securities Clearing Corporation

ISD   investment services directive (EU)

ISDA   International Swaps and Derivatives Association

IsDB   Islamic Development Bank

ISE   International Stock Exchange, *see* London Stock Exchange (LSE)

ISE/Nikkei 50 Index
Share index based on the prices of 50 Japanese equities traded both in the International Stock Exchange and on the Tokyo Stock Exchange

ISF	individual stock futures
ISG	Intermarket Surveillance Group. A group of international exchanges and regulatory authorities, whose aim is to assure the integrity of trading in options and equities, and to enhance public protection.
ISI	import-substituting industrialization
ISIC	International Standard Industrial Classification
ISIN	International Securities Identification Number
ISK	Iceland, krona (international currency symbol)
ISMA	International Securities Market Association. ISMA, founded in 1969, is the self-regulatory organization and trade association for the international securities market. For more than 500 member firms in almost 50 countries, ISMA oversees the efficient functioning of the market through the implementation and enforcement of a self-regulatory code covering trading, settlement, and good market practices.
ISMM	Institute of Sales and Marketing Management
ISO	incentive stock options
ISO	International Standardization Organization. ISO was established in 1947 and is a non-governmental federation of national standards bodies from some 140 countries worldwide, one from each country. ISO's work results in international agreements that are published as International Standards.
ISRO	International Securities Regulatory Organization
IT	income tax
IT	information technology
ITC	International Trade Centre
ITC	investment tax credit (US)
ITES	Income Tax Exemption Scheme (EU)
ITHP	increased take-home pay
ITL	Italy, lira. *Former* currency and the *former* currency of the Vatican and San Marino (international currency symbol). *Now* euro.
ITPS	Income Tax Payers' Society
ITR	Individual Turnover Report. Historic data report from the London Stock Exchange, for individual equity and fixed interest securities.
ITRE	Committee on Industry, External Trade, Research and Energy. Committee of the European Parliament.

ITS

ITS   Intermarket Trading System (US). An electronic communications network that links nine US markets.

ITU   Income Tax Unit

ITU   International Telecommunication Union. ITU was founded in Paris in 1865 as the International Telegraph Union. ITU took its present name in 1934 and became a specialized agency of the United Nations in 1947. It aims to maintain and extend international cooperation for the improvement and rational use of telecommunications of all kinds, and promote and offer technical assistance to developing countries in the field of telecommunications; to promote the development of technical facilities and their most efficient operation to improve the efficiency of telecommunication services, increasing their usefulness and making them, so far as possible, generally available to the public; to harmonize the actions of nations in the attainment of these ends.

IUMI   International Union of Marine Insurance

IVA   individual voluntary agreement. Arrangement that is legally binding between a debtor and his/her creditors in which the debtor offers the best that he/she can afford, thus avoiding bankrupt procedure costs.

IVB   invalidity benefit

IWA   International Wheat Agreement

IWC   International Wheat Council

iX   integrated exchanges

J

J$	Jamaican dollar divided into 100 cents (currency)
JA	joint accounts
J of A	*Journal of Accountancy*
JA£	Jamaican pound
JASDAQ	Japanese Association of Securities Dealers Automated Quotation System
JBL	*Journal of Business Law*
JCB	Japan California Bank
JCB	Japan Credit Bank
JCC	Junior Chamber of Commerce
JD	Jordan dinar divided into 100 fils (currency)
JDB	Japan Development Bank
JDipMA	Joint Diploma in Management Accounting Services
JDS	Joint Disciplinary Scheme
JEC	Joint Economic Committee (US Congress)
JERI	Japan Economic Research Institute
JETRO	Japan External Trade Organization
JFMIP	Joint Financial Management Improvement Programme
JGB	Japan Development Bank
JIB	Japan International Bank
JIT	Just In Time. Business management term for inventory management and purchasing system whereby materials are ordered on an as-needed basis to minimize storage and other costs and to ensure that product is as up-to-date as possible. Operation of JIT systems requires considerable cooperation between suppliers and customers.
JMD	Jamaica, dollar (international currency symbol)
JMU	Joint Monitoring Unit
JNT STK	joint stock
JOD	Jordan, dinar (international currency symbol)
JPCAC	Joint Production, Consultative and Advisory Committee
JPY	Japan, yen (international currency symbol)

JSA	Jobseeker's Allowance (UK)
JSB	joint-stock bank
JSE	Johannesburg Stock Exchange. Established in 1886, it is the largest stock exchange in Africa.
JSLB	joint stock land bank
JV	joint venture
JVI	Joint Vienna Institute (**IMF**)
J & WO	jettisoning and washing overboard (insurance)

K

K	kina divided into 100 toea (Papua New Guinea currency)
K	kwacha divided into 100 ngwee (Zambian currency)
K	kwacha divided into 100 tambala (Malawi currency)
K	Laos, kip (currency)
K	one thousand
K10	Examination paper on investment options for the Advanced Financial Planning Certificate (**AFPC**) qualification
K20	Examination paper on pension investment options for the Advanced Financial Planning Certificate (**AFPC**) qualification
KANTAFU	Kenya African National Traders' and Farmers' Union
KAP	*Kapital*. Capital. (Germany)
KC	Czechoslovakian koruna (currency)
Kcs	koruna divided into 100 halécru (Czech Republic currency)
Kcs	koruna divided into 100 halierov (Slovakian currency)
KD	Kuwaiti dinar divided into 100 fils (currency)
KES	Kenya, shilling (international currency symbol)
KG	*Kommanditgesellschaft*. Limited partnership. (Germany)
KGK	*Kabuskiki Goshi Kaisha*. Joint stock limited partnership. (Japan)
KGS	Kyrgyzstan, som (international currency symbol)
KH	Kjøbenhavns Handelsank. Copenhagen Commercial Bank, Denmark.
KHR	Cambodia, riel (international currency symbol)
KIO	Kuwait Investment Office. State-owned Kuwaiti company based in London carrying on substantial international investment.
KISS	Kurs Information Service System (Frankfurt, Germany)
KK	*Kabushi Kaisha*. Joint stock company with limited liability. (Japan)
KLCE	Kuala Lumpur Commodity Exchange. Commodity market established in 1980 for trade in rubber and crude palm oil.
KLOFFE	Kuala Lumpur Options and Financial Futures Exchange

131

KLSE	Kuala Lumpur Stock Exchange. Founded in 1973 with the ending of the joint stock exchange of Malaysia and Singapore, which had been established in 1964.
KMF	Comoros, franc (international currency symbol)
KN	Laotian kip (currency)
KN	Swedish krona (currency)
KN	Danish/Norwegian krone (currency)
KOP	Russian kopeck (currency)
KPW	Korea (North), won (international currency symbol)
KR	Icelandic krona divided into 100 aurar (currency)
KR	Swedish krona (currency)
KR	Danish/Norwegian krone (currency)
KRW	Korea (South), won (international currency symbol)
KRZL	readjusted kwanza divided into 100 lwei (Angolan currency)
KSE	Korea Stock Exchange
KSE 100	Share Index of the Karachi Stock Exchange, the principal stock exchange of Pakistan
Ksh	Kenya shilling divided into 100 cents (currency)
Kto	*Konto*. Account. (Germany)
KWD	Kuwait, dinar (international currency symbol)
KYC	know your customer. Because of public outcry regarding bank customers' privacy, US federal banking agencies withdrew these controversial regulations in 1999, which had aimed to reduce money laundering.
KYD	Cayman Islands, dollar (international currency symbol)
KYERI	know your endorsers – require identification (advice to all who cash cheques/checks)
KZT	Kazakstan, tenge (international currency symbol)

L

L	demand for money, macroeconomics symbol
L	Honduran lempira (currency)
L	Italian lira, *former* currency, *now* euro
£L	Lebanese pound (currency)
L$	Liberian dollar (currency)
LA	ledger account
LAAI	Licentiate Institute of Administration Accountants
LAB	Legal Aid Board
LAFTA	Latin American Free Trade Association. *Now* Latin American Integration Association (**LAIA**).
LAIA	Latin American Integration Association
LAK	Laos, kip (international currency symbol)
LAPFs	life assurance and pension funds
LAPR	life assurance premium relief. A tax relief given on premiums paid for life assurance policies issued in the UK up to March 1984.
LAR	life assurance relief
LAUTRO	Life Assurance and Unit Trust Regulatory Organization. Personal Investment Authority (**PIA**) since 1994.
LBC	Land Bank Commission
LBCH	London Bankers' Clearing House
LBI	Lloyds Bank International
LBMA	London Bullion Market Association
LBO	leverage buyout. Purchasing all the shares of a company by borrowing cash against the security of the shares to be bought.
LBP	Lebanon, pound (international currency symbol)
LBS	London Business School
LC	legal currency
LC	letter of credit. Letter issued by a bank authorizing the payment to a supplier; considerably used in overseas trade.

LC	Line of Credit. Bank's commitment to make loans to a particular customer up to a specified maximum amount during a specified time period.
LCB	London and Continental Bankers
LCE	London Commodity Exchange. LCE was succeeded by Futures and Options Exchange (**London FOX**) in 1987 and in turn Fox became part of London International Financial Futures Exchange (**LIFFE**) in 1996. The exchange dealt in soft commodities.
LCH	London Clearing House
LCM	lower of cost or market
LCP	least-cost planning
LD	Libyan dinar (currency)
L/D	letter of deposit
L & D	loans and discounts
L & D	loss and damage
Lda	*Sociedade de responsabilidade limitada*. Limited company. (Portugal)
LDC	less developed country. Subjective term for nation of relatively low economic strength.
LDE	London Derivatives Exchange
LDP	London daily prices
LDT	licensed deposit taker. US financial institution, other than a bank, authorized under the Banking Act 1979, and similar US legislation, to take deposits from the general public and to pay interest.
LE	Egyptian pound (currency)
Le	Sierra Leone leone (currency)
LEAPS	long-term anticipation securities
LEFTA	Labour (Party) Economic, Finance, and Taxation Association
LEL	lower earning limit (UK national insurance)
LEPO	low exercise price options
LFA	less-favoured area
LFA	Licentiate of the Institute of Financial Accountants
LFR	less-favoured region. Region having high unemployment, low domestic product per capita and low levels of economic prosperity.
L Fr	Luxembourg franc, *former* currency, *now* euro

LFS   Labour Force Survey

LGS   Loan Guarantee Scheme. Facility for encouraging the commercial banks to provide loan finance to small firms who, because of the high risk involved or lack of collateral, are unable to obtain conventional loans.

L/H   leasehold

LI   Italian lira, *former* currency, *now* euro

LIA   Life Insurance Association. Association of life insurance intermediaries founded in 1972. Its objectives are to improve professional standards, to promote knowledge and understanding of the life insurance industry, and to foster good relations with government and other bodies.

LIBA   Lloyd's Insurance Brokers' Association

LIBID   London Interbank Bid Rate. Rate of interest offered on deposits to first class banks in the London interbank market for a specific period. (**LIMEAN**: London Interbank Mean Rate – the mean of **LIBOR** and LIBID)

LIBOR   London Interbank Offered Rate. Rate of interest offered on loans to first class banks in the London interbank market for a specific period, generally three or six months. Japan has Tokyo Interbank Offered Rate (**TIBOR**) and France has Paris Interbank Offered Rate (**PIBOR**).

LIFFE   London International Financial Futures and Options Exchange. Futures market established 1982, which is engaged in the buying and selling of financial securities and commodities. LIFFE's operations have been expanded by the absorption of two other exchanges, the London Traded Options Market (1990) and the London Commodity Market (1995). LIFFE was taken over in 2001 by Euronext, an alliance of Paris, Brussels and Amsterdam stock exchanges.

LIFO   last in first out. Accountancy method of valuing stock at the price of the earliest purchases. *Also* policy that those last appointed are made redundant first.

LIMEAN London Interbank Mean Rate. The mean between London Interbank Offered Rate (**LIBOR**) and London Interbank Bid Rate (**LIBID**).

LIP   life insurance policy

LIRMA   London International Insurance and Reinsurance Market Association. International association consisting of insurance and reinsurance companies in the UK and other member countries of the European Union. (**EU**)

LKR   Sri Lanka, rupee (international currency symbol)

LL   Lebanese pound (currency)

L/L   *Lutlang*. Limited company (Norway).

LLC   Limited Liability Company

LLC   Limited Liability Corporation. Type of corporate entity, not available in all 50 of the US states, that combines the tax and legal characteristics of an organization as a corporation and as a partnership.

Llds   Lloyd's

Lloyd's   Lloyd's of London. Insurance institution founded in the 18th century by Edward Lloyd, a coffee house owner. Lloyd's is an international market for almost all types of general insurance. The capital of Lloyd's is provided by a large number of individual members each having pledged unlimited personal liability for claims.

LLP   Limited Liability Partnership. Introduced in the UK in 2000; all members share equally in the capital and profits of an LLP and every member shares in the management.

LME   London Metal Exchange. London commodity market for metals established in 1877. It trades in futures and traded options contracts for copper, primary aluminium, zinc, nickel, lead, tin, aluminium alloy, and silver.

LMEX   London Metal Exchange Index. Base metal index, weighted on the basis of world production and traded liquidity.

LMIL   London Market Information Link. The London Stock Exchange's main source of UK financial data for market professional and information vendors.

LMRA   Labor-Management Relations Act. Also know as Taft-Hartley Act, passed into US law in 1947 and the provisions of which include injunctions against labour strikes.

LMX   London Market Excess of Loss (at **Lloyd's**)

LOC   letter of credit, *see* **LC**

LOF   Lloyd's open forum

London FOX
       Futures and Options Exchange. European exchange for soft commodities (including cocoa, sugar, rubber, potatoes, and grain). It was formed in 1987 as the successor to the London Commodity Exchange. In 1996 FOX was merged with the London International Financial Futures Exchange (**LIFFE**) as a separate department.

LONRHO   London Rhodesian, a multinational company

LOTC   London over-the-counter market

L/P   life policy

LPC   Loss Prevention Council. Established in 1986, in succession to the Fire Officers Committee. Responsible for fire prevention statistics; for standard insurance policy wording; for standards of construction; for the operation of fire extinguishing appliances; for fire fighting methods in general; and for approval of equipment.

LPSO   Lloyd's Policy Signing Office

LRD   Liberia, dollar (international currency symbol)

LRR   lagged reserve requirement. US system in which banks are required to hold reserves with retrospective effect.

LRR   lower reduced rate (taxation)

LRTC   long-run total cost

LS   lump sum

LS   Syrian pound (currency)

LSA   London School of Accountancy

LSC   *Licence en Sciences Comptables*. Licentiate of Accountancy (France).

LSD   Sudanese pound (currency)

LSE   London School of Economics and Political Science

LSE   London Stock Exchange. LSE provides a marketplace where shares can be bought and sold and is one of the oldest stock exchanges in the world. In addition the LSE is responsible for vetting companies before they can be admitted to have their shares traded on a public market and it has a policing role for the market to ensure that it works efficiently and fairly. Its correct legal name is the International Stock Exchange of the UK (**ISE**).

LSE   Luxembourg Stock Exchange. The LSE is managed and self-regulated by the Société Anonyme de la Bourse.

LSL   Lesotho, loti (international currency symbol)

LTC   long term care. Insurance against the costs incurred for nursing-home accommodation or home help in old age.

LTCB   Long-Term Credit Bank (Japan)

LTCM   Long-Term Capital Management. Hedge fund that failed in 1998.

LTD   Limited. Limited liability company where shareholders are responsible for the debts of the company only for any unpaid on their shares.

LTG	leadership training graduate
LTIP	long-term incentive plan
LTL	Lithuania, lita (international currency symbol)
LTOM	London Traded Options Market. Options market merged in 1991 with the London International Financial Futures Exchange (**LIFFE**)
LTV	loan-to-value ratio
LUC	London Underwriting Centre. Centre established in 1993 for non-marine underwriters.
LUF	Luxembourg, franc (*former* currency, *now* euro), international currency symbol
LUNCO	Lloyd's Underwriters Non-Marine Claims Office
Lv	Bulgarian, lev (currency)
LVL	Latvia, lat (international currency symbol)
LYD	Libya, dinar (international currency symbol)
LYON	liquid yield option note

M

M	Lesotho loti divided into 100 lisente (pl. maloti) (currency)
M	million
M	monetary aggregate (as in **M0**, **M1**, etc.; measures of the money supply)
M1	measure of money supply, also known as "narrow money". Measure of notes and coins in circulation with the public, plus current accounts but less an allowance for items in transit.
M2	measure of money supply, also known as "broad money". M2 consists of **M1** plus savings deposits and time deposits.
M3	measure of money supply, being **M1** plus money in deposit accounts, deposits overseas currencies, money with discount houses, etc., and money deposited with banks by the public sector of the economy.
M4	UK non-bank, non-building society private sector holdings of notes and coin, plus all sterling deposits (including certificates of deposit) held at UK banks and building societies by the non-bank, non-building society private sector.
M4 lending	sterling lending by UK monetary institutions to all UK residents other than the public sector and monetary institutions. M4 lending includes loans and advances as well as investment, acceptances, and reverse repo transactions.
M$	Malaysian dollar (ringgit) divided into 100 sen (currency)
MA	machine account
MA	maternity allowance (UK)
M&A	Mergers and Acquisitions. Combination of two or more companies (merger) or the takeover by one company of the controlling interest of another (acquisition); specialized area of financial management and consulting.
MAA	Mutual Aid Association (US)
MAAT	Member of the Association of Accounting Technicians
MABRP	Member of the Association of Business Recovery Professionals
M Ac	Master of Accountancy
MAC	material adverse charge

MACB   Marine Association of Community Banks (US)

MACHA   Mid-Atlantic Clearing House Association (US)

MAD   Morocco, dirham (international currency symbol)

MAFR   merged accountability and fund reporting

MAI   Member of the Appraisal Institute

M-AID   Marshall Aid. Financial aid given to European countries by USA under Marshall Plan. Plan originally proposed by General George Marshall in 1947.

MANF   May, August, November, February (end dates for quarterly payments)

MAP   modified American plan (payment system in US hotels)

MAPA   Members' Agents Pooling Arrangement (Lloyd's)

MAPS   MidAmerica Automated Payments System (US)

MAQ   Mortgage Advice Qualification

MAR   marginal age relief (taxation)

MASP   monthly average settlement price

MAT   marine, aviation, and transport. Recognized class of insurance business.

MATIF   Marché à Terme des Instruments Financiers. French financial futures exchange, established in 1986. *Also* known as Marché à Terme International de France.

Mau Re   Mauritian rupee (currency)

MB   Merchant Bank. European or US financial institution that offers services that include investment banking, portfolio management, mergers and acquisitions, and accepting deposits generated by bank credit/debit and charge card transactions.

MBA   Master of Business Administration

MBA   Mortgage Bankers of America

MBAG   Mortgage Bankers Association of Georgia (US)

MBB   mortgage-backed bonds

MBC   Mercantile Bank of Canada

mbH   *mit beschränkter Haftung*. With limited liability (company). (Germany)

MBI   management buy-in. Purchase of a company by outside directors.

MBIM   Member of the British Institute of Management

MBM   Master of Business Management

MBO   management buy-out. Acquisition of all or part of the share capital of a company by its directors and senior executives.

MBO   management by objectives. Approach to management, popularized by American management writer Peter Drucker, which emphasizes the need for clear organizational objectives that can be incorporated in the actions of individual managers.

MBS   Manchester Business School

MBS   mortgage backed securities

MBWA   management by walking around. Approach to management that emphasizes the value of observing what goes on in the organization and of displaying a high profile to subordinates.

MC   Marketing Council

M/C   marginal credit

MCA   Management Consultants Association

MCA   married couple's allowance. Tax allowance abolished in 2000 (UK)

MCA   monetary compensatory amount

MCAs   monetary compensatory amounts. Also known as green money. The system used by the Common Agricultural Policy (**CAP**) of the European Community to convert the common prices agreed for farm products into the national currencies of those member countries which are not converted to the euro and to realign prices when the exchange rates of those currencies change.

MCB   Member of British Association of Communicators in Business

MCBSI   Member of the Chartered Building Societies Institute

MCCB   Mortgage Code Compliance Board

MCIBS   Member of the Chartered Institute of Bankers in Scotland

MCIM   Member of the Chartered Institute of Marketing

MCIPD   Member of the Chartered Institute of Personnel and Development. Corporate membership is available to graduate members who can demonstrate three years' relevant experience at management level and appropriate continuing professional development.

MCIPS   Member of the Chartered Institute of Purchasing and Supply

MCIS   Member of the Institute of Chartered Secretaries and Administrators

MCT   mainstream corporation tax

MCT   Member of the Association of Corporate Treasurers

MDA   mid-cap index. German stock exchange index listing 70 German companies.

MDFC   McDonnell Douglas Finance Corporation

MDL   Moldova, leu (international currency symbol)

MDO   monthly debt ordinary

MEB   Master of European Business

M Econ   Master of Economics

MECU   Municipal Employees Credit Union

Medicare   Medical Care. The US Social Security Act (1965) provides, through Medicare, federally funded health insurance coverage for the elderly and handicapped.

MEFF   Mercado Español de Futuros Financieros. Spanish futures and options exchange.

MEP   Member of the European Parliament

MERC   Chicago Mercantile Exchange

MERCOSUR

Mercado Común del Sur. Southern (American) Common Market. Founded in March 1991 by the Treaty of Asunción between Argentina, Brazil, Paraguay, and Uruguay, the treaty committed the signatories to the progressive reduction of tariffs culminating in the formation of a common market on 1 January 1995.

MESBIC   minority enterprise small business investment companies

MEW   measure of economic welfare

MEW   mortgage equity withdrawal

Mex$ Mexican peso (currency)

MFA   Managed Funds Association

MFA   Multi-Fibre Arrangement. Trade pact between some 80 developed and developing countries, which regulates international trade in textiles and clothing through the use of quotas on imports. Its purpose is to give poor countries guaranteed and growing access to markets in Europe and North America, but at the same time to ensure this growth does not disrupt the older established textile clothing industries of the developed countries.

MFC   marginal factor cost. Extra cost incurred by a firm in using one more unit of a factor input. Marginal factor cost together with the marginal revenue product of a factor, indicates to a firm how many factor inputs to employ in order to maximize its profits.

MFN   most forward nation (in trade agreements)

MFOA   Municipal Finance Officers Association

MFR   minimum funding requirement. UK regulation for company pension funds.

M/G   *mi giro*. My check/cheque; my draft. (Spanish)

MGF   Madagascar, franc (international currency symbol)

MGFr   Malagasy franc (Madagascan currency)

MGFV   minimum guaranteed future value

MIAB   Member of the International Association of Book-keepers

MIAM   Member of the Institute of Administrative Management

MIAS   Member of the Institute of Accounting Staff

MIATI   Member of the Institute of Accounting Technicians in Ireland

MIBA   Missouri Independent Bankers Association (US)

MIB (Scot)   Member of the Institute of Bankers in Scotland

MICB   Member of the Institute of Certified Book-keepers

MICM   Vocational Member of the Institute of Credit Management

MICM (Grad)
Graduate Member of Institute of Credit Management. Associate members (AICM) who have completed the Institute's Diploma qualification.

MICR   magnetic ink character recognition. Magnetic ink is used on documents such as cheques enabling them to be automatically sorted and characters read and fed into a computer.

MICS   Member of the Institute of Chartered Shipbrokers

MIEM   Master in International Economics and Management

MIF   Mercato Italiano Futuri. Italian futures market

MIFF   Member of the Institute of Freight Forwarders

MIG   minimum income guarantee

MIG   mortgage indemnity guarantee

MIGA   Multilateral Investment Guarantee Agency. Established in 1988 to encourage the flow of foreign direct investment to, and among, developing countries. MIGA is the insurance arm of the World Bank (**WB**). It provides investors with investment guarantee against non-commercial risk, such as expropriation and war, and gives advice to governments on improving climate for foreign investment.

143

MIJ	*Maatschapij*. Netherlands joint stock company.
MIMC	Member of the Institute of Management Consultants
MIMgt	Member of the Institute of Management
MInstSMM	Member of the Institute of Sales and Marketing Management
MIP	marine insurance policy
MIP	maximum/monthly investment plan
MIPA	Member of the Insolvency Practitioners Association
MIPS	monthly income preferred security
MIR	mortgage interest relief
MIRAS	mortgage interest relief at source. Arrangement whereby interest payments on a mortgage used to purchase or improve a person's home are allowed against that person's income tax. This arrangement was cancelled in April 2000. (UK)
MIS	management information systems
MIS	Master in Information Systems
MIT	Massachusetts Investors Trust
MITI	Ministry of International Trade and Industry (Japan)
MJD	management job description
MK	Finnish markka divided into 100 pennia (currency)
MK	Malawi kwacha (currency)
MKD	Macedonia, denar (international currency symbol)
MLR	minimum lending rate. Lowest interest rate at which the Bank of England will discount approved bills of exchange to relieve shortages in the money market. MLR replaced bank rate in 1972 but the Bank of England discontinued the system in 1981.
MMAS	Manufacturing Management Accounting System
MMB	Marine Midland Bank
MMBA	Massachusetts Mortgage Bankers' Association (US)
MMC	Monopolies and Mergers Commission. The Commission was established in 1948 as the UK Monopolies and Restrictive Practices Commission and later became MMC. In 1999 it was renamed the Competition Commission (**CC**) and its task is to investigate and report on matters referred to it by the Secretary of State for Trade and Industry or the Director-General of Fair Trading, or by the regulators of regulated utilities. It has no power to initiate investigations. (UK)

MMDA   Money Market Deposit Account. Highly liquid, market-sensitive bank account available since 1982, with an interest rate generally comparable to rates on money-market mutual funds, and insured by the Federal Deposit Insurance Corporation.

MMI   Major Market Index. Share index measuring the average prices of 20 major industrial stocks quoted on the New York Stock Exchange. Developed by the American Stock Exchange in 1983.

MMI   major money index. Futures contract established by the Chicago Board of Trade in 1983 and based on movements in the Dow-Jones Industrial Average Index of the stock exchange prices of 30 of the most heavily capitalized companies in the USA.

MMK   Myanmar (Burma), kyat (international currency symbol)

MMMFs   money-market mutual funds

MMOB   Military Money Order Branch

MMS   Member of the Institute of Management Services

MMU   million monetary units

MNC   multinational company. Firm that owns production, sales and other revenue-generating assets in a number of countries.

MNC   multinational corporation

MNE   multinational enterprise. Firm that owns production, sales and other revenue-generating assets in a number of countries.

MNT   Mongolia, tugrik (international currency symbol)

MO   notes and coins in circulation outside the Bank of England and bankers' operational deposits at the Bank

MOF   multiple option facility

MOMS   *mervaerdiomsaetningskat*. Value-added tax. (Denmark)

MOMS   *mervardesomsattningskatt*. Value-added tax (Sweden)

MONEP   Marché des Options Négotiables de Paris. French traded options market, established in 1987 and is a subsidiary of the Paris Bourse.

MOO   money order office

MOP   Macau, pataca (international currency symbol)

MORI   Market and Opinion Research International. As in "Mori poll".

MORT   mortgage

MOTA   Mail Order Trade Association

M & P   Ministry of Pensions and National Insurance. In UK, was merged with the National Assistance Board to form the Ministry of Social Security.

MPA   Master of Professional/Public Accounting

MPA   Metropolitan Pensions Association

MPC   Monetary Policy Committee. Bank of England committee responsible for arranging UK interest rates to facilitate and encourage growth compatible with low inflation. Established by the 1998 Bank of England Act, the MPC consists of the Governor and the two Deputy Governors of the Bank, two members appointed by the Bank after consultation with the Chancellor, and four members appointed by the Chancellor. A representative of the Treasury attends meetings in a non-voting capacity. The MPC meets monthly. Decisions are announced immediately after the meeting and the minutes are published two weeks later.

MPX   Mid-American Payment Exchange (US)

Mpy   *Maatschappij*. Company. (Netherlands)

MQA   marketing quality assurance

MRD   mutual recognition directive (EU)

MRe   Mauritian rupee (currency)

MRO   Mauritania, onguiya (international currency symbol)

MRP   manufacturer's recommended price

MRP   marginal revenue product

MRP   materials requirement planning. Planning system for scheduling stock replenishments so as to ensure that adequate amounts of materials are available at all times thus enabling production to go ahead without interruption.

MRRP   manufacturer's recommended retail price

MRVA   Member of the Rating and Valuation Association

M/S   months after sight

MSA   Master Senior Appraiser

MSB   Marketing Standards Board

MSc ECON
               Master of Science in Economics

MSCI   Morgan Stanley Capital International. Market index includes about 23 individual markets covering 65 per cent of market capitalization, expressed in US dollars, of the world stock exchanges.

MSCI Index
Morgan Stanley Capital International World Index

MSE   Manila Stock Exchange. Established in 1927, one of three stock exchanges in the Philippines.

MSE   Midwest Stock Exchange

MSE   Montreal Stock Exchange

MSF   Manufacturing, Science and Finance. Trade Union, an amalgamation of ASTMS (Association of Scientific, Technical, and Managerial Staffs) and TASS (Technical, Administrative, and Supervisory Staffs). (UK)

MSFA   Member of the Society of Financial Advisers

MSI   Member of Securities Institute

MSP   matched sale-purchase agreement. Sale of money-market instruments by the US Federal Reserve for immediate effect, coupled with a forward purchase of the same instruments.

MSRB   Municipal Securities Rulemaking Board

MSRP   manufacturer's suggested retail price (US)

MT   Mozambique metical divided into 100 centavos (currency)

MTA   minimum terms agreement

MTFA   medium-term financial assistance. Loans of a term of two to five years, available from EU countries to a member country experiencing balance of payments difficulties.

MTFS   medium-term financial support

MTGEE   mortgagee

MTGOR   mortgagor

MTL   Malta, lira (international currency symbol)

MTN   medium term note. Unsecured note issued in a euro-currency with a maturity of three to six years.

MTO   Multilateral Trade Organization

MTP   Maltese pound (*former* currency, *now* lira)

MU   monetary unit

MUCPI   Monetary Union Consumer Price Index, which is based on the Harmonized Consumer Price Index (HCPI) of the member states and produced by EUROSTAT.

MUR   Mauritius, rupee (international currency symbol)

MVA   market value added

MVA   market value adjuster

MVA   market value appraiser

MVL

MVL	members' voluntary liquidation
MVR	Maldives, rifiyaa (international currency symbol)
MWCA	monetary working capital adjustment
MWK	Malawi, kwacha (international currency symbol)
MXP	Mexico, peso (international currency symbol)
MYR	Malaysia, ringgit (international currency symbol)
MYRA	Multi-Year Rescheduling Agreement. Arrangement, first instituted in 1985, for the postponement to various years of the due dates for repayment of loans from commercial banks to developing countries.
MZM	Mozambique, metical (international currency symbol)

N

N	Bhutan ngultrum (currency)
₦	Nigerian naira (currency)
N$	Namibian dollar (currency)
N2	Date, 1 December 2001, when the Financial Services Authority **(FSA)** acquired its powers under the Financial Services and Markets Act
N30	net (payment) in 30 days
NA	new account
N/A	no account
N/A	non-acceptance
NAAACPA	National Association of Asian-American Certified Public Accountants
NAAI	National Association of Accountants in Insolvencies
NAB	national advisory board
NAB	National Association of Businessmen (US)
NAB	National Australia Bank
NAB	New Arrangement to Borrow **(IMF)**
NABA	National Association of Black Accountants
NACA	National Association of Consumer Advocates
NACHA	National Automated Clearing House Association (US)
NACIMFP	National Advisory Council on International Monetary and Financial Problems
NAD	Namibia, dollar (international currency symbol)
NAEFTA	National Association of Enrolled Federal Tax Accountants
NA f	Netherlands Antillean guilder (currency)
NAFC	National Accounting and Financial Council
NAFCU	National Association of Federal Credit Unions
NAFTA	North America Free Trade Agreement. Regional free trade area established in 1989 between USA and Canada; extended to include Mexico in 1994. It aims to remove trade barriers for most manufactured and agricultural goods, and raw materials over a period of ten years. Restrictions on investment, banking, and financial services across borders would also be reduced or removed.

NAG   net annual gain

NAIC   National Association of Investment Clubs

NAIL   New Africa Investments Limited (South Africa)

NAIRU   non-accelerating inflation rate of unemployment

NAMSB   National Association of Mutual Savings Banks

NAO   National Audit Office. The role of the Comptroller and Auditor General, as head of the National Audit Office, is to report to Parliament on the spending of central government money. The Office conducts financial audits of all government departments and agencies and many other public bodies, and reports to Parliament on the value of money with which public bodies have spent public money. Relations with Parliament are central to the work, and the Office works closely with the Committee of Public Accountants. It also works closely with other public audit bodies who have a role in other areas of public expenditure. (UK)

NAPF   National Association of Pension Funds. Organization for providers of occupational pension schemes. (UK)

NAPM   National Association of Purchasing Management, *now* Institute for Supply Management (US)

NAR   National Association of Realtors. The NAR has nine affiliated institutes, societies, and councils that provide a wide-ranging menu of programmes and services to assist members in increasing skills, productivity, and knowledge. Designations acknowledging experience and expertise in various real estate sectors are awarded by each affiliated group on completion of required courses. In addition, NAR offers two certification programmes to its members. (US)

NAREIF   National Association of Real Estate Investment Funds

NASA   National Association of Securities Administrators

NASAA   North American Securities Administrators Association. National association of individuals who administer securities laws of the US states and the Canadian provinces.

NASBA   National Association of State Boards of Accountancy

NASCUS   National Association of State Credit Union Supervisors

NASD   National Association of Securities Dealers. New York-based organization for standards and ethical behaviour composed of investment banking firms and supervised by the Securities and Exchange Commission (**SEC**). NASD monitors the over-the-counter (**OTC**) market.

NASDAQ   National Association of Securities Dealers Automated Quotation system. NASDAQ International is a service established in 1971 and is a screen-based quotation system supporting market-making in US registered equities. NASDAQ International has operated from London since 1992.

NASDAQ EUROPE
A stock exchange, in Brussels, for technology and growth companies based in Europe. *Formerly* known as the European Association of Securities Dealers Automated Quotations (**EASDAQ**), it is modelled on **NASDAQ** in the USA, who hold a 58 per cent stake.

NASPA   National Association of Public Accountants (US)

NATA   National Association of Tax Administrators (US)

NatWest   National Westminster Bank

NAV   net asset value

NBA   National Bankers' Association

NBA   National Banking Association

NBAD   National Bank of Abu Dhabi

NBD   National Bank of Detroit

NBE   National Banker Examiner(s)

NBER   National Bureau of Economic Research (US)

NBG   National Bank of Georgia

NBG   National Bank of Greece

NBK   National Bank of Kuwait

NBNZ   National Bank of New Zealand

NBSA   National Bank of South Africa

NBV   net book value

NC   Norske Creditbank. Norwegian Credit Bank.

N/C   no charge

NCA   National Credit Association

NCB   National Central Banks (EU)

NCCF   National Commission on Consumer Finance (US)

NCFA   National Consumer Finance Association (US)

NCH   National Clearing House

NCI   New Community Instrument. Loan financed by direct international borrowing of the European Commission.

NCPS   non-contributory pension scheme

NCSC   National Companies and Securities Commissions (Australia)

NCT   National Chamber of Trade

N/CTA   *nuestra cuenta*. Our account. (Spanish)

NCUA   National Credit Union Administration. Regulates all US credit unions and insures credit union deposits up to $100,000.

NCUA   National Credit Union Association

NCUP   no commission until paid

NCUSIF   National Credit Union Share Insurance Fund

NCV   no commercial value

ND   national debt

ND   next day

NDB   National Development Bank

NDCs   National Debt Commissioners. The eight NDCs are the Chancellor of the Exchequer, the Governor and both Deputy Governors of the Bank of England, the Speaker of the House of Commons, the Master of the Rolls, the Accountant General of the Supreme Court, and the Lord Chief Justice. (UK)

NDF   Nordic Development Fund. Established in 1989, the NDF is a development aid organization of the five Nordic countries, Denmark, Finland, Iceland, Norway and Sweden. Credits are offered to under-developed countries, with African, Asian, and Latin American countries taking priority.

NDO   National Debt Office. The origins of the NDO were in the passing of the National Debt Reduction Act of 1786. Although there had been numerous earlier attempts to set up sinking funds to reduce the National Debt, they all suffered from the defect that the monies could be applied towards defraying current expenditure and inevitably, they were sooner or later diverted to that purpose.

By the early 1780s however, strong pressure was being exerted on the government to ensure that positive steps were taken to reduce and, eventually, eradicate the National Debt. The 1786 Act appointed six Commissioners for the Reduction of the National Debt, and they were authorized to employ such clerks and other officers as were necessary, thereby establishing the National Debt Office. (UK)

NDP   net domestic product

NDPB	non-departmental public body
NE	no effects (i.e. no funds)
N/E	not entered
NEACH	New England Automated Clearing House (US)
NEB	National Enterprise Board (UK), replaced by the British Technology Group (**BTG**)
NEC	National Economic Council (US)
NEDC	National Economic Development Council, also known as Neddy (UK)
NEDO	National Economic Development Office (UK)
NEO	non-equity options
NESTA	National Endowment for Science, Technology, and the Arts (UK)
NEW	net economic welfare (US)
NF	no funds
NFA	National Futures Association. NFA is the self-regulatory organization for the US commodity futures industry, authorized by the US Congress in 1974, NFA is a membership organization comprised of individuals and entities in the business of placing futures and commodity options trades at exchanges on behalf of their customers. NFA's activities are overseen by the Commodity Futures Trading Commission (**CFTC**), the government agency responsible for regulating all aspects of the US commodity futures industry. CFTC registration is a prerequisite for NFA membership.
NFA	non-food agriculturals. Commodity price index.
NFB	Nippon Fudosan Bank. Japan Real Property Bank.
NFC	Navy Finance Center (US)
NFCC	National Foundation for Consumer Credit
NFCSA	National Finance Corporation of South Africa
NFU	National Farmers' Union. Association representing employers in agriculture. (UK)
NGN	Nigeria, naira (international currency symbol)
NGO	non-governmental organization. Interest groups, companies, consumer groups, and trade unions that influence policy within the **EU** and the **UN**.
NHS	National Health Service

NIB Nordic Investment Bank. NIB is the joint international financial institution of the Nordic countries. It commenced operations in 1976 and finances investment projects and project exports both within and outside the Nordic area. Priority is given to investment and environmental loans for projects in the Baltic States, Poland, and northwest Russia.

NIBA National Introducing Brokers Association (US)

NIBA Nebraska Independent Bankers Association (US)

NIC National Institute of Credit

NIC national insurance contributions

NIC National Investors Council

NIC newly industrialized country. Country that has not yet achieved the status of an advanced country, but is no longer a developing or Third World country. They include South Korea, Singapore, and Taiwan.

NIC Nicaraguan córdoba (currency)

NIEO New International Economic Order

NIESR National Institute of Economic and Social Research

NIF note issuance facility. Medium-term Eurocredit under which the borrower issues a series of short-term instruments against a banker's guarantee over the whole term, given in the form of either an underwriting or a back-up credit arrangement.

NIFA Network of Independent Forensic Accountants

NIFO next in first out. Goods held in stock at end of accounting period in which the replacement value of the goods is used and not the original (historical) cost.

NIL National Investment Library

NILO National Investment and Loans Office. Formed on 1 April 1980 as the outcome of a merger of the staffs of the National Debt Office (**NDO**) and the Public Works Loan Board (**PWLB**). In 2002 it merged with the Debt Management Office (**DMO**). (UK)

NIMEXE Nomenclature of goods for the external trade statistics of the EC and statistics of trade between member states. Replaced by the Combined Nomenclature (**CN**).

NINO national insurance number (UK)

NIO Nicaragua, córdoba oro (international currency symbol)

NIRA National Industrial Recovery Act (US)

NIS New Independent States (former States of the Soviet Union)

NIT	negative income tax
NKz	new kwanza (Angolan currency)
NLDF	National Lottery Distribution Fund (UK)
NLF	National Loans Fund
NLG	Netherlands, guilder (*former* Dutch currency, *now* euro), international currency symbol
NMC	National Marketing Council
NMC	no more credit
NM COM	*nemine contradicente*. Without opposition.
NMS	National Market System (US)
NMS	normal market size
NMW	national minimum wage
NN & EB	National Newark & Essex Bank
NNP	net national product
NO	no orders
No	number
NOA	not otherwise authorized
NOK	Norway, krone (international currency symbol)
NOL	net operating loss
NOM CAP	nominal capital

NOW account

Negotiable Order of Withdrawal account. Personal interest-bearing savings account at a bank or savings and loan association on which a negotiable order of withdrawal may be drawn.

NP	new pence. Introduced in UK in 1971.
NP	note payable
N/P	nil paid
NPB	National Provincial Bank, *now* **NatWest**
NPR	Nepal, rupee (international currency symbol)
NPV	net present value
NPV	new present value
NPV	no par value
NRDC	National Research and Development Corporation (UK). Replaced by British Technology Group (**BTG**).
NRs	Nepalese rupee (currency)

NRFC	Navy Regional Finance Center (US)
NROR	normal rate of return
NRT	net registered tonnes
NRV	net realizable value
NS	National Savings. *Now* National Savings and Investments (**ns&i**).
N/S	not sufficient
NSA	National Society of Accountants
NSB	National Savings Bank. British savings bank administered by the Department of National Savings and operating through the post office network. *Formerly* known as the Post Office Savings Bank.
NSCC	National Securities Clearing Corporation. Organization through which brokerage firms, exchanges, and other clearing corporations reconcile accounts with each other.
NSE	National Stock Exchange (India). Established in 1994 by the Indian government with headquarters in Bombay.
NSF	not sufficient funds
ns&i	National Savings and Investments. Until 2002 National Savings (UK).
NSM	National Savings Movement
NSO	nonqualified stock options
NSPA	National Society of Public Accountants
NSSR	National Savings Stock Register
NT$	new Taiwan dollar (currency)
NTA	net tangible assets
NTBs	non-tariff barriers. Obstacles to trade other than quotas and tariffs, such as safety or construction regulations which favour domestic over imported products; legal requirements that providers of insurance services should be domiciled within national boundaries and deliberate delay or obstruction at customs.
NTDA	National Trade Development Association
NTDB	National Trade Data Bank. International trade data bank compiled by 15 US government agencies. The data bank contains the latest census data on US imports and exports by commodity and country, the complete *CIA World Factbook*, and current market research among others.
NTEU	National Treasury Employees Union (US)

NTIATA	National Tax Institute of America Tax Association
NTLC	National Tax Limitation Committee
NT & SA	National Trust and Savings Association (US)
NU	Bhutan ngultrum (currency)
NUIW	National Union of Insurance Workers
Nur$	Uruguayan new perso (currency)
NV	*Naamloze Vennootschap*. Dutch public limited company.
NV	non-voting
N/V	no value
NVA	net value added
NVCA	National Venture Capital Association (US)
NW	net worth
NW CHA	Northwest Clearing House Association (US)
NYCE	New York Cotton Exchange
NYFE	New York Futures Exchange
NYMEX	New York Mercantile Exchange. Commodity market founded, under its present name, in 1887 dealing in futures of crude and heating oil, leaded petrol (gasoline), platinum, and palladium.
NYSBB	New York State Banking Board
NYSE	New York Stock Exchange. NYSE was established in 1792 and is the oldest and largest stock exchange in the US. Also called The Big Board and The Exchange.
NZ$	New Zealand dollar divided into 100 cents (*also* the currency of Cook Islands, Niue, Tokelau, and Pitcairn Islands)
NZD	New Zealand, dollar (international currency symbol)
NZFOE	New Zealand Futures and Options Exchange. Established in 1985. Exchange trading in financial futures, currencies, and wool using an automated trading system. The NZFOE is owned by the Sydney Futures Exchange (**SFE**).
NZLR	*New Zealand Law Reports*
NZSE	New Zealand Stock Exchange

O

OA	old account
OA	on account
O & A	October and April (on bills)
OAC	on approved credit
OAP	old age pension(er)
OAPEC	Organization of Arab Petroleum Exporting Countries. Established in 1968 to promote cooperation and close ties between member states in economic activities related to the oil industry; to determine ways of safeguarding their legitimate interests, both individual and collective, in the oil industry; to unite their efforts so as to ensure the flow of oil to consumer markets on equitable and reasonable terms; and to create a favourable climate for the investment of capital and expertise in their petroleum industries. Members are Algeria, Bahrain, Egypt, Iraq, Kuwait, Libya, Qatar, Saudi Arabia, Syria, Tunisia, and United Arab Emirates. Tunisia's membership was made inactive in 1986.
OAS	option-adjusted spread
OAT	Obligation Assimilable du Trésor. French treasury bill.
OBO	Office of the Banking Ombudsman
OBO	or best offer
OBSF	off balance sheet finance
OBSO	Office of the Building Societies Ombudsman
OBU	offshore banking unit
OBX	Oslo Børs. Oslo Stock Exchange.
OCBC	Overseas Chinese Banking Corporation
OCC	Office of the Comptroller of the Currency. Bureau of the US Treasury Department designed to safeguard bank operations and the public interest through its general supervision over the operations of national banks.
OCC	Options Clearing Corporation
OCDE	Organisation de Coopération et de Développement Économiques. Organization for Economic Cooperation and Development.
O/D	on demand

O/D	overdraft
O/D	overdrawn
OECD	Organization for Economic Cooperation and Development. In 1961 the Organization for European Economic Cooperation (**OEEC**) was replaced by the Organization for Economic Cooperation and Development (OECD). With the accession of Canada and the USA as full members it ceased to be a purely European body and added development aid to the list of its activities. Objectives are to promote economic and social welfare throughout the OECD area by assisting its member governments in the formulation of policies designed to this end and by coordinating these policies, and to stimulate and harmonize its members' efforts in favour of developing countries.
OECE	Organisation Européenne de Coopération Économique. Organization for European Economic Cooperation, *now* **OCDE**.
OECS	Organization of Eastern Caribbean States. Founded in 1981 when seven eastern Caribbean states signed the Treaty of Basseterre agreeing to cooperate with each other to promote unity and solidarity among the members. It aims to promote cooperation among members and to defend their sovereignty, territorial integrity, and independence.
OEEC	Organization for European Economic Cooperation. Organization established in 1948 in response to the offer of Marshall Aid from the USA. Open to all European countries, membership comprised 17 nations of Western Europe; the Eastern European countries, including the Soviet Union, refused to join. In 1961 OEEC was replaced by the Organization for Economic Cooperation and Development (**OECD**).
OEEO	Office of Equal Employment Opportunity. Subsidiary of the US Department of Labor.
OEIC	open-ended investment company. Investment fund that is very similar to a unit trust, with a single buying and selling price. Instead of units an OEIC issues shares. (Often pronounced "oiks".)
OEO	Office of Economic Opportunity (US)
OEP	Office of Economic Preparedness (US)
OFCs	other financial corporations
OFDI	Office of Foreign Direct Investments
OFEX	Off exchange. An unregulated alternative to the official stock market.

OFLOT	Office of the National Lottery (UK)
OFPM	Office of Fiscal Plans and Management
OFR	operating and financial review
OFT	Office of Fair Trading. UK authority established by the Fair Trading Act, 1973, to administer all aspects of UK competition policy, specifically the control of monopolies, mergers and takeovers, restrictive trade agreements, resale prices, and anticompetitive practices.
OGL	open general licence
OGM	ordinary general meeting
OHBMS	On Her/His Britannic Majesty's Service
OHG	*Offene Handelsgesellschaft*. Partnership. (Germany)
OHMS	On Her/His Majesty's Service
OICA	Ontario Institute of Chartered Accountants
OIEC	Organization for International Economic Co-operation
OIEO	offers in excess of
OIO	Office of the Investment Ombudsman
OIS	Overseas Investors Services
OJAJ	October, January, April, July (months for quarterly payments)
OJT	on-the-job training
OKB	Oesterreichische Kontrolbank. Semi-official Austrian financial institution, supported by government funds, issuing bonds in particular in the international and **Eurobond** markets.
OM	Swedish options market. Options market opened in 1989 by Options Market London Exchange (**OMLX**) in conjunction with the Swedish options market, trading in Swedish and Norwegian equity derivatives.
O & M	organization and methods
OMA	orderly marketing agreement
OMB	Office of Management and Budget. US federal government agency responsible for assisting the President in preparing the budget and formulating the fiscal programme of the US government.
OMF	Office of Management and Finance
OMFP	obtaining money by false pretences
OMLX	Options Market London Exchange

160

OMO	open market operation
OMR	Oman, rial (international currency symbol)
OMS	output per man shift
OMV	open-market value
ONGC	Oil and Natural Gas Commission (US)
ONO	or near offer
ONS	Office for National Statistics. UK government department that collects and publishes statistics concerning the economy, such as the National Income *Blue Book*.
OOPEC	Office for Official Publications of the European Communities
OP	open policy
OPAB	Occupational Pensions Advisory Board
OPAS	Occupational Pensions Advisory Service
OPB	Occupational Pensions Board
OPCS	Office of Population Censuses and Surveys
OPE	out-of-pocket expenses
OPEC	Organization of Petroleum Exporting Countries. Inter-governmental organization of oil-producing countries, established in 1960. In the 1960s the member countries nationalized the management of the oilfields, until then operated by the major international oil companies. In 1973 the OPEC countries reduced output and embargoed supplies to Western countries, with a sharp increase in oil prices. By the mid-1980s because of energy conservation, and the opening of major new oilfields, the OPEC domination of prices ended.
OPEIU	Office and Professional Employees International Union (US)
OPG	Office of Her Majesty's Paymaster General
OPIC	Overseas Private Investment Corporation. US government agency established to encourage US private investment in emerging countries.
OPL	overall premium limit. Maximum amount of insurance a member of Lloyd's can underwrite.
OPM	Office of Personnel Management (US)
OPM	other people's money
OPRA	Occupational Pensions Regulatory Authority. Established by the UK parliament to help make sure that occupational pensions schemes are safe and well run. It can impose penalties where there are breaches of the law, for example if trustees do not appoint advisers or keep proper records.

OR	Official Receiver
OR	Oman, rial divided into 1000 baizas (currency)
OR	owner's risk (insurance)
ORF	owner's risk of fire (insurance)
ORR	Office of the Rail Regulator
OSC	Ontario Securities Commission
OSE	Osaka (Japan) Stock Exchange
OTC	over-the-counter market. Market for corporate shares that have not obtained a full listing on the main stock market. The UK's OTC market was abolished in 1992. Sometimes called the Third Market. *See* Alternative Investment Market (**AIM**).
OTE	on-target-earnings. Salary a salesperson should be able to achieve.
OTOB	Oesterreichische Termin und Optionsbörse. Futures and options market. (Austria)
OTS	Office of Thrift Supervision. Bureau of the Department of the Treasury that charters federal savings institutions and serves as primary regulator for federal and state chartered savings institutions that belong to the Savings Institutions Insurance Fund (**SIIF**).
OVPD	overpaid
OXERA	Oxford Economic Research Associates. Economic consultants specializing in economic and financial analysis.

P

P	penny
₱	Philippine peso (currency)
P	Spanish peseta, *former* currency, *now* euro
P	Botswana, pula divided into 100 thebe (currency)
P2P	path to profitability
PA	particular average (insurance)
PA	payment appropriations (EU)
PA	per annum. In a year.
PA	personal accident
PA	personal allowance (taxation)
PA	power of attorney
PA	public accountant
P/A	paid annually
P/A	personal account
P/A	private account
PAB	Panama, balboa (international currency symbol)
PAB	Price Adjustment Board
PAC	Public Accounts Committee
PAC	put-and-call (option)
PACB	Pennsylvania Association of Community Bankers (US)
PACE	performance and cost evaluation
Pak Re	Pakistan, rupee (currency)
PAQ	professional accountancy qualifications
Paribas	Banque de Paris et des Pays-Bas (France)
PAT PEND	patent pending
PAYE	pay-as-you-earn. Scheme for collecting income tax due from the earnings of an individual by deducting the tax owing before an employer pays wages or salaries. PAYE is not a tax, merely a scheme for the collection of tax.
PAYE	pay as you enter
PAYG	pay as you go (pensions)

PB	passbook. Document provided by a bank or building society showing balance held after a deposit or withdrawal
PBGC	Pension Benefit Guarantee Corporation (US)
PBIT	profit before interest and tax
PBP	pay-back period. Amount of time required for the cumulative estimated future income from an investment to equal the amount initially invested.
PBPS	programme budgeting and planning system
PBR	payment by results
PBR	pre-budget report (UK)
PBT	pay-back time
PBT	profit before tax
PBWSE	Philadelphia-Baltimore-Washington Stock Exchange
PC	paycheck
PC	petty cash
PC	price current
PCARS	Point Credit Accounting and Reporting System
PCB	Pensions Compensation Board
PCB	petty cash book
PCB	private car benefits
PCG	Professional Contractors' Group
PCM	per calendar month
PCP	permissible capital payment
PCP	personal contract purchase
PCPI	Permanent Committee on Patent Information (*see* **WIPO**)
PCTCT	profit chargeable to corporation tax
PD	postage due
PD	post-dated. Check, letter, invoice, or document dated later than the date on which it was actually written.
P/D	price-dividend
P/D ratio	price-dividend ratio
PDVSA	Petroleos de Venezuela. State-owned oil company of Venezuela.
P/E	plant and equipment
P/E	price-earning ratio. Present market price of an ordinary share divided by the company's net earnings per share,

usually after tax. It gives an investor an estimate of how much they are paying for a company's earning power.

PEA primary expense account

PEFA Private Equity Funding Association

PEFCO Private Export Funding Corporation

PEG FACTOR

prospective earnings ratio. Factor used to indicate the relative attraction, and consequent value-enhancing potential, from investing in a growth company.

PEN Peru, nuevo sol (international currency symbol)

Penny Benny

see **ERISA**

PEP personal equity plan. Scheme launched by the UK government in 1987, to provide tax relief on the proceeds of personal investment in equities listed on the stock exchange. In any one year a maximum of £6000 per annum plus £3000 in a single company PEP per individual could be invested. There is no tax on capital gains, and dividends are free of income tax if reinvested. **ISA**s replaced PEPs in April 1999.

PER Price-earning ratio. Present market price of an ordinary share divided by the company's net earnings per share, usually after tax. It gives an investor an estimate of how much they are paying for a company's earning power.

PERC preferred equity redemption stock

PERLS Principal Exchange-Rated-Linked Securities

PER PRO *per procurationem*. With the authority of.

PERT programme evaluation and review technique. Also known as network analysis. A method of planning, scheduling, and controlling projects involving interrelated but distinct elements of work or activities.

PES Peruvian nuevo sol (currency)

PESC Public Expenditure Survey Committee

PETs Potentially exempt transfers. Gifts between individuals are termed PETs for tax purposes. A PET made at least seven years before death becomes an exempt transfer. If death occurs within seven years then the gift becomes taxable subject to taper relief.

PF pfennig (former German currency)

Pf pfennig (former German currency)

PF public funding

PF	public funds
PFC	privately financed consumption
PFD	preferred
PFI	private finance initiative. UK government-sponsored programme of public-sector construction project in which financing costs are shared with private-sector enterprises.
PFP	personal financial planning
PFPUT	Pension Fund Property Unit Trust
PFS	Personal Finance Specialist
PGK	Papua New Guinea, kina (international currency symbol)
PHI	permanent/private health insurance
PHLX	Philadelphia Stock Exchange
PHP	Philippines, peso (international currency symbol)
PI	personal income
P & I	principal and interest
PI	profitability index
PIA	Personal Investment Authority. Self regulatory organization for the regulation of retail financial products. The PIA replaced **FIMBRA** and **LAUTRO** and some activities of **IMRO** and the **SFA** in 1994 and has itself been absorbed into the **FSA**.
PIAOB	Personal Investment Authority Ombudsman Bureau. Now part of the **FSA**.
PIAS	Personal Insurance Arbitration Service
PIB	Prices and Incomes Board
PIBOR	Paris Interbank Offered Rate. French equivalent of **LIBOR**.
PIBS	permanent interest-bearing shares. Form of investment in a building society.
PIC	professional investment certificate
PIC	ProShare Investment Clubs
PICC	People's Insurance Company of China. Important state-run insurance company.
P & I clubs	protection and indemnity clubs. Mutual associations first founded in the early 19th century to provide protection to shipowners against risks not normally covered by conventional marine insurance. Members pay an annual levy or "call" determined by the tonnage of the vessel concerned.

PIF Pacific Islands Forum. In October 2000 the South Pacific Forum changed its name to the Pacific Islands Forum. As the South Pacific Forum it held its first meeting of Heads of Government in New Zealand in 1971. The PIF provides an opportunity for informal discussions to be held on a wide range of issues. It meets annually or as necessary. The Forum has no written constitution or international agreement governing its activities nor any formal rules relating to its purpose, membership, or conduct of its meetings. Its mission is to enhance the economic and social wellbeing of the South Pacific peoples, in support of the efforts of the national governments. Members are Australia, Cook Islands, Fiji, Kiribati, Marshall Islands, Micronesia, Nauru, New Zealand, Niue, Palau, Papua New Guinea, Samoa, Solomon Islands, Tonga, Tuvalu, and Vanuatu. In 1999 the French territory of New Caledonia was admitted to the Forum as an observer.

PIK payment-in-kind bond

PIMA **PEP** and **ISA** Managers' Association

PIN personal identification number. Number, generally selected by the customer, used to access funds or account information electronically from cash dispensers.

PINC property income certificate. Share in the ownership of a single building, giving holders the benefits of income and capital growth, but which can be traded.

PIPPY person inheriting parents' property

PIS perpetual inventory system. Stock control system avoiding closing stockrooms for annual stock checks. Records show items purchased and items sold so that figures on the stock records are accurate and up-to-date.

PITI principal, interest, taxes, insurance

PIX Finnish wood-pulp price index

PK banken Post-och Kreditbanken. Post and Credit Bank. (Sweden)

PKR Pakistan, rupee (international currency symbol)

P/L partial loss (insurance)

P & L profit and loss account. Financial statement showing revenue, expenditure, and the profit or loss resulting from operations in a given period.

plc public limited company. Unofficial variants are p.l.c., PLC, P.L.C., Plc. (UK)

PLOM prescribed loan optimization model

PLP personal leasing plans

PLR	Public Lending Right. Established in 1983 PLR is a scheme where payment is made from public funds to authors whose books are lent out from public libraries. The term "author" includes writers, illustrators, translators, and some editors/compilers. (UK)
PLZ	Poland, złoty (international currency symbol)
PM	premium
PMI	private medical insurance
PMI	private mortgage insurance
PMI	Purchasing Management's Index
PMT	payment
PMT	post-market trading. Automated screen trading system operated by the Chicago Mercantile Exchange in collaboration with Reuters.
PMTS	predetermined motion-time standards
P/N	promissory note
PNFCs	private non-financial corporations
PO	Pensions Ombudsman
PO	postal order
PO	principal only
PO	purchase order
POD	pay(ment) on delivery
POD	Post Office Department (US)
POL ECON	political economics/economy
POO	post office order
POP	proof of purchase
POPA	Property Owners Protection Association
POR	pay on receipt/payable on receipt
POR	pay on return
POS	point-of-sale
POSA	payment outstanding suspense accounts
POSB	Post Office Savings Bank
POTAM	Panel on Takeovers and Mergers. POTAM regulates conduct of takeovers and mergers in the UK.
P & P	payments and progress

P & P   post and packing

PPBES   planning-programming-budgeting-evaluation system

PPI   policy proof of interest

PPI   producer price indices. PPI measure the changes in prices charged by businesses "at the factory gate" for the goods they produce and are an alternative measure of inflation.

PPP   public private partnership (UK)

PPP   purchasing power parity. Exchange rates based on the relative prices of the same basket of goods in each country.

PPR   permanent pay record

PPS   prescribed payments system (Australia)

PR   preferred stock

PR   public relations. General means of promoting a business's company image with a view to encouraging customers to buy its products and investors to buy its shares, as well, for example, as influencing government policies on issues relevant to the company.

PRO NOTE

promissory note

ProShare   Independent, non-profit-making organization established to encourage and support individual investment in the stock market by private individuals. It provides information and assistance to investment clubs. ProShare lobbies government and the relevant industry bodies to ensure that individual investment operates in a suitable tax and regulatory framework. It provides teaching material and runs The National Investment Programme for Schools and Colleges in which teams research and manage imaginary portfolios of shares. ProShare provides assistance to companies with employee share schemes or those interested in establishing them. It works closely with companies and suppliers to promote best practice in employee share ownership.

PRP   performance-related pay

PRP   profit-related pay. System in which all or some of an employee's wage or salary is directly based on or related to company profitability. The total level of pay will therefore vary in relation to movements in profitability.

PRT   petroleum revenue tax. Tax on the profits of oil companies. Originally introduced to increase tax from the profits on the development of oilfields in the North Sea. (UK)

P & S   purchase and sale (US)

PSA	Prices Surveillance Authority (Australia)
PSA	Public Securities Association
PSAC	Policy Signing and Accounting Centre
PSB	Postal Savings Bureau (Japan)
PSB	Premium Savings Bond
PSBR	public-sector borrowing requirement. Excess of government expenditure over taxation receipts, requiring the government to make good the difference by borrowing money from the banking system (Treasury bills) or from the general public (long-date bonds).
PSCA	Profit-Sharing Council of America (US)
PSDR	public sector debt repayment. Excess of taxation receipts over government expenditure enabling the government to use the difference to repay past borrowings.
PSDR	public sector debt requirement
PSE	Pacific Stock Exchange. Regional stock exchange, based in Los Angeles and San Francisco, that handles trading on the West Coast.
PSFS	Philadelphia Savings Fund Society
PSHFA	Public Servants Housing Finance Association
PSI	Present Situation Index. Measures consumer perceptions of current economic conditions.
PSL	private sector liquidity
PSL	public sector loan(s)
PSNB	public sector net borrowing
PSNCR	public sector net cash requirement
PSO	Professional Standards Office
PSR	profit-sharing ratio
PSRF	Profit Sharing Research Foundation
PT	perfect title. Generally referred to as clear title, indicating that title to a property is free of disputed interests.
PTA	Spanish peseta, *former* currency, *now* euro
PTE	Portugal, escudo (*former* Portuguese currency, *now* euro), international currency symbol
Pte	Private limited company (India, Singapore)
PTO	Public Trustee Office
PTP	publicly traded partnership

PTPG   participating

PTS   payments

PTS   private trading system. Screen-based trading system used by institutional investors and broker-dealers not wishing to use the stock exchanges on grounds of cost, secrecy, or other reasons.

Pty   Proprietary Company (Australia and South Africa). Also used in the USA for an insurance company owned by outside directors.

PUC   Public Utilities Commission (US)

PUHCA   Public Utility Holding Company Act (US)

PV   par value

PV   present value

PVBP   price value of a basis point

PWA   postwar credits

PWC   PricewaterhouseCoopers (accountants)

PWLB   Public Works Loan Board. British government institution established to provide loan finance to local authorities, often at lower rates of interest than those obtainable in the capital market. The origins of the Public Works Loan Board may be traced back to an Act of 1793, which set up a body known as the Exchequer Loan Commissioners to lend up to £5 million by means of short-term Exchequer Bills. This Act was followed by several others in subsequent years, each setting up an ad hoc body of Commissioners to make short-term loans for some specific purpose. The most interesting was the appointment in 1795 of Commissioners empowered to lend to people connected with or trading to the islands of Grenada and St Vincent in view of losses sustained in insurrections. As security they were empowered to take mortgages on the plantations, including the black slaves employed on the estates. Became part of the National Investment and Loans Office (**NILO**) in 1980.

PYB   preceding-year basis

PYG   Paraguay, guarani (international currency symbol)

Q

Q	bankruptcy or receivership (stock exchange symbol)
Q	Guatemalan quetzal divided into 100 centavos (currency)
QA	quality approval
QAR	Qatar, rial (international currency symbol)
QC	quality control
QCA	Quoted Companies Alliance
QCS	quality cost system
QLF	quality loss function
QMV	qualified majority voting (EU)
QSSR	quarterly stock status report
QUANGO	quasi-autonomous non-government organization. Executive body which is responsible for overseeing a designated area of public sector activities and spending.
QUEST	quarterly European simulation tool. Modelling project of the Economic and Financial Affairs of the European Commission to link quarterly econometric models for the individual member states and Japan. (EU)
QWL	quality of working life

R

R	South African rand divided into 100 cents (currency)
R	rate of interest
R	rupee (currency)
R$	Brazilian real divided into 100 centavos (currency)
R/A	refer to acceptor (on a bill of exchange)
RAA	Residential Accredited Appraiser
RADARS	Receivable Accounts Data-entry and Retrieval System
RAFT	revolving acceptance facility by transfer
RAM	Reverse Annuity Mortgage. Mortgage loan that allows the homeowner-borrower (generally elderly) to live off the substantial equity in the property.
RAO	Regulated Activities Order
RAP	Regulatory Accounting Principles
RAS	Report Audit Summary
RASG	*ragioniere*. Accountant. (Italy)
RBA	Reserve Bank of Australia
RBC	Royal Bank of Canada
RBI	Reserve Bank of India
RBL	Russian ruble (currency)
RBN	Registry of Business Names
RBNZ	Reserve Bank of New Zealand
RCA	regulatory capital arbitrage
RCA	Replacement Cost Accounting. Practice of valuing assets and property at replacement value.
RCH	recognized clearing house
RCIA	Retail Credit Institute of America
RCT	receipt
R/D	refer to drawer (on a cheque)
R&D	research and development. Commitment of resources by a firm to scientific research.
RD$	Dominican Republic peso divided into 100 centavos (currency)
RDB	Regional Development Bank

R/E	rate of exchange
REBAC	Real Estate Buyer's Agent Council
REC	Recruitment and Employment Confederation
RECD	received
RECS	Real Estate Cyberspace Specialist
REDS	Refunding Escrow Deposits. Financial instruments that lock in a lower current rate in anticipation of maturing higher-rate issues by way of a forward purchase contract that obligates investors to buy bonds at a predetermined rate when they are issued at a future date that coincides with the first optional call date on existing high-rate bonds. In the interim, investors' money is invested in Treasury Bonds, bought in the secondary market, which are held in escrow, effectively securing the investor's deposit and paying taxable annual income. The Treasuries mature around the call date on the existing bonds, thereby providing the money to buy the new issues and redeem the old one.
REF	reference
ref	refund(ing)
REG	EU Regulation that automatically becomes law in all the member states
REIT	real-estate investment trust. Publicly quoted trusts issuing bonds secured by commercial property. (US)
Remitt	remittance
REPO	sale and repurchase agreement. Transaction whereby funds are borrowed through the sale of short-term securities on the condition that the instruments are repurchased at a given date. *Also* REPOS.
RERC	Real Estate Research Corporation. Chicago-based organization that undertakes independent research projects on trends and opportunities within the real estate industry.
REV	revenue
Rf	Maldivian rufiyaa (currency)
RFQ	request for quotation
R FR	Rwanda franc(s) (currency)
RFS	Registry of Friendly Societies
RGNP	real gross national product
RHM	*RHM Survey of Warrants, Options & Low-Priced Stock.* Weekly publication which provides investment advice on warrants, call and put options, and low-priced stocks.

RI   residual income

RIA   Registered Investment Adviser. According to the Securities and Exchange Commission, any individual registered under the Investment Advisers Act of 1940, who, for compensation, engages in the business of advising others as to the value of securities or as to the advisability of investing in, purchasing, or selling securities.

RICO   Racketeer Influenced and Corrupt Organizations Act. US congressional law enacted in 1970 to deal with organized crime's infiltration of legitimate business.

RICS   Royal Institution of Chartered Surveyors

RIE   Recognized Investment Exchange. Body that meets the minimum criteria laid down by the Financial Services Act. RIEs are COREDEAL, **IPE**, JIWAY, **LIFFE**, **LME**, **LSE**, **OMLX**, and **VIRT-X**. (UK)

RIMBA   Rhode Island Mortgage Bankers Association (US)

RITC   reinsurance to close. A Lloyd's syndicate must, before it closes at the end of the year, provide for the payment of any claims that may subsequently arise from the policies it has written. (Lloyd's syndicates have a legal life for one year.) It therefore reinsures against this with the reconstituted syndicate, paying a premium for this into the account of that syndicate, as reinsurance to close.

RL   Russian ruble (currency)

RLS   Iranian rial (currency)

RM   Reichs-mark, former German currency

RM   Malaysian ringgit (currency)

RMA   Risk Management Association

RMACHA   Rocky Mountain Automated Clearing House Association (US)

RMB   Chinese renminbi (currency)

RNB   received, not billed

RNS   Regulatory News Service of the London Stock Exchange (**LSE**). RNS ensures that price sensitive information from listed and Alternative Investment Market (**AIM**) companies, and certain other bodies, is disseminated to all RNS subscribers at the same time.

RO   Omani rial (currency)

ROA   received on account

ROA   Reinsurance Offices Association

ROA   return on assets

ROAM   return on assets managed

ROCE   return on capital employed. Rate of return that the company's management has obtained on the shareholders' behalf through management of the company's assets.

ROE   return on equity

ROI   return on investment. Financial ratio giving the percentage profit of total assets or capital employed.

ROL   Romania, leu (international currency symbol)

ROM   results-oriented management

RONA   return on net assets

RP   Swiss rappen (or centime) (currency)

RP   recommended price

RP   redundancy payment

RP   repurchase agreement

RP   Indonesian rupiah divided into 100 sen (currency)

RPA   Real Property Administrator

RPB   recognized professional body. RPBs are Chartered Association of Certified Accountants, Institute of Actuaries, Institute of Chartered Accountants in England and Wales, Institute of Chartered Accountants in Ireland, Institute of Chartered Accountants in Scotland, Insurance Brokers Registration Council, the Law Society, the Law Society of Ireland, and the Law Society of Scotland.

RPC   Restrictive Practices Court. Regulatory body responsible, in part, for the implementation of UK competition policy. The basic task of the RPC is to investigate and report on cases of restrictive trade agreements, information agreements, and resale price maintenance referred to it by the Office of Fair Trading (**OFT**) to determine whether or not they operate against the public interest.

RPI   Retail Price Index. RPI is used to show the level of inflation and its effect on the cost of living. The average price of a "basket" of everyday goods and services is used to give an index figure. It aims to measure changes in the cost of living.

RPI INFLATION
inflation measured by the retail price index (**RPI**)

RPIX   retail price index excluding mortgage interest payments

RPIX INFLATION
> inflation measured by the **RPI** excluding mortgage interest payments

RPIY INFLATION
> inflation measured by the **RPI** excluding mortgage interest payments and indirect taxes

RPM　　resale price maintenance. Type of restrictive trade practice whereby a supplier prescribes the price at which all retailers are to sell the product to final buyers. The practice of RPM was made illegal in the UK in 1964 except for some trades such as bookselling and pharmacies. These restrictions have now been abolished.

RPPP　　relative purchasing power parity

RPQ　　request for price quotation

R & R　　reconstruction and renewal (**Lloyd's**)

RRM　　renegotiable-rate mortgage (US)

RRP　　recommended retail price. Indicates a manufacturer's recommendation to retailers of pricing for a given item of merchandise.

RS　　Mauritius rupee divided into 100 cents (currency)

RS　　Seychelles rupee divided into 100 cents (currency)

Rs　　Indian rupee divided into 100 paisas (currency)

Rs　　Nepalese rupee divided into 100 paisas (currency)

Rs　　Pakistan rupee divided into 100 cents (currency)

Rs　　Sri Lankan rupee divided into 100 cents (currency)

RSP　　Retail Service Provider. One of the four UK firms that aggregate private investor trades for dealing via **SETS**.

RTA0　　reciprocal trade agreement

RTB　　Rural Telephone Bank(ing)

RTC　　Resolution Trust Corporation

RTC　　revenue and taxation code

RTK　　right to know

RTS Index　　Russian Trading System Index. Share price index of the Moscow Central Stock Exchange.

RUF　　revolving underwriting facility

RUR　　Russia, ruble (international currency symbol)

RWF　　Rwanda, franc (international currency symbol)

S

S	schilling, *former* Austrian currency, *now* euro
S	sen (Japanese currency)
S	shilling. British currency until 1971, equivalent to five pence.
S	silver
S	sol (Peruvian currency)
S	stock
S	Ecuador, sucre (currency)
S	surplus
S2P	state second pension
S$	Samoan tala divided into 100 sene (currency)
S$	Singapore dollar divided into 100 cents (currency)
S£	Syrian pound divided into 100 piastres (currency)
SA	Securities Association
SA	*Sociedad anonima*. Public limited company. (Portugal)
SA	*Sociedade anonima*. Public limited company. (Spain)
SA	*Società anonima*. Public limited company. (Italy)
SA	*Société anonyme*. Belgian/French limited company. Also used in some non-French-speaking countries, e.g. Greece.
SA	Society of Actuaries, *also* S of A
S/A	survivorship agreement (US)
SA£	South African pound, *former* currency, *now* Rand
SA$	Samoan tala (currency)
SAA	strategic asset allocation
SAARC	South Asian Association for Regional Co-operation. SAARC was established in August 1983 with the objectives of promoting the welfare of the peoples of South Asia; to accelerate economic growth, social progress and cultural development; to promote and strengthen collective self-reliance among members; to promote active collaboration and mutual assistance in the economic, social, cultural, technical, and scientific fields; and to strengthen cooperation with other developing countries, and among themselves through inter-

national forums on matters of common interest. Cooperation within the framework is based on respect for the principles of sovereign equality, territorial integrity, political independence, non-interference in the internal affairs of other states, and mutual benefit. Members are Bangladesh, Bhutan, India, Maldives, Nepal, Pakistan, and Sri Lanka.

SAC   short-run average cost

SAC   Standards Advisory Council

SAC   statistical advisory committee

SADC   South African Development Community. SADC was formed in 1980 under the name Southern African Development Co-ordination Conference (**SADCC**) and aims to promote economic integration and strengthen regional solidarity, peace and security.

SADCC   Southern African Development Co-ordination Conference

SAE   *Société Anonyme Egyptienne*. Egyptian limited company.

SAEF   Stock Exchange Automatic Execution Facility. Computerized system for executing small purchase and sales orders for shares on the London Stock Exchange.

SAF   Structural Adjustment Facility. Established in 1986 to provide assistance to low-income countries. (**IMF**)

SAIF   Savings Association Insurance Fund

SAL   salary

Sallie Mae   *see* **SLMA**

SAM   shared-appreciation mortgage

SAMA   Saudi Arabian Monetary Agency

SANPAOLO
Instituto Bancario San Paolo di Torino. San Paolo Banking Institute of Turin. (Italy)

SANZ   Standards Association of New Zealand

SAP   structural adjustment programme

SAPCO   single asset property company

SAR   Saudi Arabia, riyal (international currency symbol)

SAR   stock appreciation right

SARL   *Sociedade anonima de responsabilidade limitada*. Joint stock limited liability company. (Portugal)

SARL   *Société à responsabilité limitée*. Private limited company. (France)

SAS	*Società in accomandita semplice.* Limited partnership. (Italy)
SASs	Statements of Auditing Standards. *See* Appendix 5.
SAV	sale/stock at valuation
SAV	statement of value added
SAYE	save as you earn
SB	savings bank
SB	short bill
SB	small business
SB	Standard Brands (stock exchange symbol)
SBA	School of Business Administration
SBA	Small Business Administration. US government agency providing management and financial assistance to businesses that lack the resources to pursue capital and other advantages available to larger corporations.
SBC	Small Business Council
SBC	Swiss Bank Corporation
SBD	Solomon Islands, dollar (international currency symbol)
SBF	Société des Bourses Françaises. Association of French Stock Exchanges.
SBI	State Bank of India
SBIC	small business investment company. Company set up with low-cost funds and taxation advantages from the US federal government to invest in small businesses, authorized under the Small Business Investment Act 1958.
SBLA	Small Business Loans Act. Canadian legislation providing government funding for small business owners.
SBLI	Savings Bank Life Insurance (US)
SBSA	Standard Bank of South Africa
SCA	shared-cost action
SCA	*Société en commandité par actions.* French/Belgian company partnership limited by shares.
SCAN	stock market computer answering network
SCANS	Stockmarket Computer Answering Service
SCAPA	Society for Checking the Abuses of Public Advertising
SCARF	systems control and review file
SCB	Solicitor Complaints Bureau
SCC	Stock Clearing Corporation

SCCA   Scottish Consumer Credit Association

SCCA   Society of Company and Commercial Accountants

SCE   Standing Committee on Employment

SCIT   Special Commissioners of Income Tax

SCM   smaller companies market. The third-tier unlisted securities market (**USM**) in Ireland. Ireland also has a second-tier USM.

SCMC   Société de Compensation des Marchés Conditionnels. French equity options market operator.

SCNE   Select Committee on National Expenditure

SCOBEC Scottish Business Education Council

SCOTIABANK
           Bank of Nova Scotia

SCOUT shared currency option under tender

SCR   scrip

SCR   Seychelles, rupee (international currency symbol)

SCREAM Society for the Control and Registration of Estate Agents and Mortgage Brokers

SCWS   Scottish Cooperative Wholesale Society

SD   Diploma in Statistics

SD   safe deposit

SD   sight draft

SD   Sudanese dinar divided into 10 pounds (currency)

S/D   sight draft

SDA   severe disablement allowance (UK)

SDB   sales day book

SDBL   sight draft bill of lading

SDD   Sudan, dinar (international currency symbol)

SDDA   Special Data Dissemination Standard. Established in 1996 to improve access to reliable economic statistical information for member countries that have, or are seeking, access to international capital markets. (**IMF**)

SDMJ   September, December, March, June (dates for quarterly payments)

SDP   Sudanese pound (currency)

SDR   Special Drawing Right. Monetary asset held by member countries of the International Monetary Fund (**IMF**) as part of their international reserves. Unlike other reserve assets such as gold, SDRs have no tangible life of their own. They are "created" by the IMF itself and take the form of book-keeping entries in a special account managed by the Fund. The SDR was formerly valued in terms of a weighted basket of five currencies: US dollar, German deutschmark, UK sterling, French franc, and Japanese yen.

SDRT   stamp duty reserve tax

SE   Scottish Enterprise. Founded in 1991 its purpose is to create jobs and prosperity for the people of Scotland. It is funded by the Scottish Executive and is responsible to the Scottish Ministers.

SE   self-employed. Earning one's living directly from one's own profession or business, as opposed to as an employee earning salary, commissions, or wages.

SE   Stock Exchange

SEA   Single European Act. SEA was signed in February 1986, and aimed to amend and expand the three original treaties of the European Community. Member states stated that it was their intention to "transform relations ... among their States into a European Union". Two important changes were the abolition of the right to veto, i.e. the substitution of majority voting for unanimous voting on proposed legislation, on all subjects except taxation, free movement of people and the "rights and interests of employed persons"; and greater involvement of the European Parliament in the lawmaking process.

A major element of the Single Act was a commitment to complete the unification of the internal market. It aimed to build on the European Monetary System (**EMS**) leading to Economic and Monetary Union (**EMU**), and a project for a European central bank and an eventual common currency was envisaged. Also included was a "social charter" (**ESC**) stating the rights of workers, signed in 1989 by all member states except the UK.

SEA   Southern Economic Association

SEAF   Stock Exchange Automated Exchange Facility

SEAQ   Stock Exchange Automated Quotation System. Screen-based quotation system for securities that allows market makers on the London Stock Exchange to report their price quotes and trading volumes to users of the system. SEAQ was introduced in the preparation for the "Big Bang" and has allowed all transactions on the exchange to be carried out by telephone rather than as formerly on the trading floor.

SEAQ INTERNATIONAL
Stock Exchange Automated Quotations System for international equities

SEATS   Automated screen trading system on the Australian Stock Exchange

SEATS   Stock Exchange Alternative Trading Service. System for trading less liquid securities introduced on the London Stock Exchange on 16 November 1992 to replace the Company Bulletin Board, where there is only either a single or no market maker. The screen displays the current quotations for the market maker (if any) and current public orders to provide a central point for business in these illiquid stocks. SEATS complements the Stock Exchange Automated Quotations Systems (**SEAQ**).

SEB   Skandinaviska Enskilda Banken. Scandinavian Loan Bank.

SEBI   Securities and Exchange Board of India. The regulator of stock exchange in India.

SEC   Securities and Exchange Commission. US government agency that regulates the activities of stockbrokers and traders in securities, protecting the investing public against malpractice in securities investment. It also promotes full public disclosure and monitors takeovers in the US. Should a person or organization acquire five per cent or more of equity of another company it is obliged to notify SEC.

SECMA   Stock Exchange Computer Managers Association

SEDOL number
Stock Exchange Daily Official List number. UK quoted securities are given a SEDOL number. This number also serves as the International Securities Identification Number (**ISIN**).

SEHK   Stock Exchange of Hong Kong. In 1984 the four stock exchanges in Hong Kong were unified and became the Stock Exchange of Hong Kong.

SEK   Sweden, krona (international currency symbol)

SELA   Sistema Economico Latin-americano. Latin American Economic System, founded 1975. SELA promotes coordination on economic issues and social development among the countries of Latin America and the Caribbean. Its members are Argentina, Bahamas, Barbados, Belize, Bolivia, Brazil, Chile, Colombia, Costa Rica, Cuba, Dominican Republic, Ecuador, El Salvador, Grenada, Guatemala, Guyana, Haiti, Honduras, Jamaica, Mexico, Nicaragua, Panama, Paraguay, Peru, Suriname, Trinidad and Tobago, Uruguay, and Venezuela.

SEM   Single European Market

SenC   *Sociedad en commandita*. Limited partnership. (Spain)

SenC   *Société en commandité*. Limited partnership. (France)

SenCN   *Société en non collective*. Partnership. (France)

SEP   selective employment payments

SEPON   Stock Exchange Pool Nominees. Official UK stock market company which receives details of all stocks and shares transfers, and facilitates prompt settlement of account and transfer of share certificates, making use of the **CREST** computerized transfer system.

SERP   Self-Employed Retirement Plan. Tax-deferred pension plan for self-employed individuals and employees of small, unincorporated businesses, also called Keogh Plan.

SERPS   state earnings-related pension scheme

SES   Stock Exchange of Singapore

SESDAQ   Stock Exchange of Singapore Dealing and Automated Quotation System

SESI   Stock Exchange of Singapore Index

SET   Securities Exchange of Thailand. Established in 1975 to succeed the Bangkok Stock Exchange.

SET   Selective Employment Tax/Taxation. UK tax started in 1966 but abolished when VAT was introduced in 1973.

SET   settlement

SETS   Stock Exchange (Electronic) Trading System. Order driven electronic system, SETS, based on the new trading and information platform called Sequence, was introduced in 1997, initially for the **FTSE 100** Index Companies and applied to orders over £4000.

SF   *sans frais*. Without expense. (French)

SF   sinking fund. Any amounts put aside to reduce total indebtedness, but particularly to reduce the British national debt. First introduced in 1717.

S&F   stock and fixtures (insurance)

SFA   Securities and Futures Authority. Authority responsible for regulating the conduct of brokers and dealers in securities, options and futures. *Now* part of the Financial Services Authority (**FSA**).

SFAC   Social Fund Advisory Committee

SFAC   Statement of financial accounting concepts

SFACB	Securities and Futures Authority Complaints Bureau
SFAS	Statement of Financial Accounting Standards. Rule of accounting practice developed and issued by the Financial Accounting Standards Board (**FASB**). *See* Appendix 6.
SFE	Southern Financial Exchange (US)
SFE	Sydney Futures Exchange. Trades financial futures, including contracts based on the All Ordinaries Index, and other futures and options, including commodity futures such as wool and live cattle. The SFE also owns the New Zealand Future and Options Exchange (**NZFOE**).
SFFAS	Statements of Federal Financial Accounting Standards. Official promulgations by the US Federal Accounting Standards Advisory Board (**FASAB**).
SFI	*Société financière internationale*. International Finance Corporation.
SFO	Serious Fraud Office. Government department engaged in investigating major fraud within companies.
SFO	Superannuation Funds Office
SFR	sinking fund rate of return
SFSE	San Francisco Stock Exchange
SFT	specified financial transactions
SGB	Société Générale de Banque. Belgian Bank.
SGD	Singapore, dollar (international currency symbol)
SH	share
SHARP	Shareholder Appreciation Right Program (US)
SHB	Svenska Handelsbanken. Swedish Bank.
Sh F	shareholders' funds
SHP	Saint Helena, pound (international currency symbol)
SHR	share
SI	Securities Institute. Professional body for UK securities and investments. Chiefly for stockbrokers. Established 1992.
SI	statutory instrument
SI	sum insured
SI	Système International d'Unités. International Measurement System.
SI$	Solomon Islands dollar divided into 100 cents (currency)
SIA	Securities Industry Association (US)

SIA	Society of Industrial Accountants. Canadian trade organization.
SIA	Society of Industrial Analysts
SIA	Society of Insurance Accountants
SIAC	Securities Industry Automation Corporation. US corporation providing automation, data-processing, and communication facilities for the National Securities Clearing Corporation, a clearing house jointly owned by the New York Stock Exchange (**NYSE**), the American Stock Exchange (**ASE**) and the National Association of Securities Dealers (**NASD**), set up in 1977.
SIAS	Statement on internal auditing standards
SIB	Savings and Investment Bank
SIB	Securities and Investment Board. *Former* agency established under the Financial Services act 1986 for regulating the activities of investment businesses in the UK. *Now* the Financial Services Authority (**FSA**).
SIBOR	Singapore Inter-Bank Offered Rate
SIC	Standard Industrial Classification
SIC	Standing Interpretations Committee
SICA	Society of Industrial and Cost Accountants
SICA	Society of Industrial and Cost Accountants of Canada
SICAV	*Société d'investissement à capital variable*. French unit trust.
SIECA	Secretaria de Integración Económica Centroamericano. Secretariat for Central American Economic Integration. SIECA was established in 1952 when the five member states formed a Committee for Economic Co-operation of the Central American Isthmus. Members are Costa Rica, El Salvador, Guatemala, Honduras, and Nicaragua. Observer: Panama.
SIIF	Savings Institutions Insurance Fund
SIMAP	Système d'Information pour les Marchés Publics. EU system to promote, coordinate and manage change in public procurement. Set up under the **IDA** programme to access international procurement databases.
SIMEX	Singapore International Monetary Exchange. Deals in financial (especially Eurodollar), energy and commodity futures. SIMEX was established in 1984 and now has a mutual offset arrangement with the Chicago Mercantile Exchange.
SIMP	statutory illustration of money purchase. From April 2003 all money purchase schemes for pensions in the UK will have

to send out an annual statement with standard illustrations projecting the pension income on retirement. Unlike current projections, these illustrations will have to take into account inflation, and show the annual income in today's money.

SIOR   Society of Industrial and Office Realtors. Individuals certified with the SIOR designation are top producers in industrial and office real estate brokerage, representing more than 800 offices in over 350 cities worldwide. The Society's mandatory recertification requirement assures clients of the designee's excellence in the fast changing commercial brokerage field.

SIP   Society of Investment Professionals

SIP   supplemental income plan

SIPC   Securities Investor Protection Corporation. Compensation scheme in the USA for investors in the event of the failure of market makers or dealers. All members of the National Association of Securities Dealers (**NASD**) belong to SIPC.

SIPP   self-invested personal pension

SIR   small income relief

SIR   Statement of Investment Circular Reporting Standard

SIRE   Small Investors Real Estate

SIT   Slovenia, tolar (international currency symbol)

SITC   Standard International Trade Classification. United Nations classification. *A Guide to the Classification of Overseas Trade Statistics* is published annually.

SITS   Securities Instruction Transmission System

SKK   Slovakia, koruna (international currency symbol)

SKU   stock-keeping unit

S & L   Sale and Leaseback or Sale-Leaseback. Simultaneous purchase of real estate and lease back to the seller, generally on a long-term lease. The seller-lessee receives the proceeds of the sale while retaining occupancy of the property. *Also* S/L.

S & L   savings and loan associations. US savings banks that receive savings deposits and make mortgages. They are referred to as savings and loan institutions and thrifts, they exercise some banking functions, such as operating cheque/checking accounts, and provide consumer credit and high-yield investment vehicles. S & Ls are largely mutual organizations, though many have been incorporated so as to broaden their access to capital markets. S & Ls are regulated either by the Federal Home Loans Bank Board or, in the case of state chartered S & Ls, by the state.

S & L	savings and loan banks
SLIC	Savings and Loan Insurance Corporation (US)
SLL	Sierra Leone, leone (international currency symbol)
SLMA	Student Loan Marketing Association. Established by the US Higher Education Act of 1965, also known as **Sallie Mae**.
SMEs	small- and medium-sized enterprises (EU)
SMF	Securities Masterfile. Provides up-to-date information on securities traded on UK and international markets.
SMI	Swiss-Market Index. Leading exchange index of the Swiss Stock Exchange.
SMITES	State-Municipal Income Tax Evaluation System
SMP	statutory maternity pay (UK)
SNA	*System of National Accounts*. Publication containing macro-economic accounts, issued by EUR-OP for **EUROSTAT** in 1993.
SNB	sellers no buyers
SNIF	short-term note issuance facility
SNIG	sustainable noninflationary growth
SO	standing order
S/O	seller's option
Soc	*società*. Company. (Italy)
SOC	Standard Occupational Classification. Issued in the UK by the Office for National Statistics, and in the US by the Federal Office of Management and Budget.
SOC ACHA	South Carolina Automated Clearing House Association (US)
SOCRED	Social Credit
SOES	Small Order Execution System (of **NASDAQ**)
SOFA	Society of Financial Advisers
SOFFEX	Swiss Options and Financial Futures Exchange. Options and futures market established in 1988 by the Basle, Geneva, and Zürich stock exchanges, together with five Swiss banks. Trading began in options on up to 15 first-line Swiss stocks.
SOLACE	Sales Order and Ledger Accounting (using) Computerline Environment
SOLV	solvent
SOP	statement of position
SORP	statement of recommended practice

SOS	Somalia, shilling (international currency symbol)
SP	statement of practice
SP	stop payment
S&P	Standard and Poor's. US company that provides a broad range of investment services, primarily rating bonds and stocks, and compiling indexes and publishing statistics, advisory reports and financial information. The S&P or Poor's 500 measures price changes in 500 securities quoted on the New York Stock Exchange (**NYSE**); 400 company stocks, 40 financial, 20 transportation, and 40 public utility issues are included.
SpA	*Società per Azioni.* Italian public corporation. The corporation must have at least two shareholders at formation.
SPA	state pension age. Age at which men and women become eligible for pensions provided by the state.
SPA	sundry persons account
SPARTECA	South Pacific Regional Trade and Economic Cooperation Agreement
SPC	Secretariat of the Pacific Community. Intergovernmental organization founded in 1947 under an Agreement commonly referred to as the Canberra Agreement. It is funded by assessed contributions from its 27 members and by voluntary contributions from member and non-member countries, international organizations and other sources. Its three main areas of work are land resources, marine resources and social resources. It conducts research and provides technical assistance and training in these areas to member Pacific Island countries and territories of the Pacific. Members are American Samoa, Australia, Cook Islands, Fiji, France, French Polynesia, Guam, Kiribati, Marshall Islands, Federated States of Micronesia, Nauru, New Caledonia, New Zealand, Niue, Northern Mariana Islands, Palau, Papua New Guinea, Pitcairn Island, Samoa, Solomon Islands, Tokelau, Tonga, Tuvalu, UK, USA, Vanuatu, and Wallis and Futuna.
SPD	subject to permission to deal
SPDA	single-premium deferred annuity
SPDR	Standard & Poor's Depositary Receipt. SPDRs track the value of the S & P's 500 Composite Price Index.
SPI	selected period investment
SPNB	Security Pacific National Bank
SPOT	single property ownership trust

SPQR	small profits and quick returns
SPRL	*Societé de personnes à responsabilité limitée*. Limited company. (France)
SR	short rate
SR	standard rate
S/R	sale or return
SRA	Senior Residential Appraiser
SRAC	short-run average cost
SRB	sales returns book
SRC	*Sociedad regular collectiva*. Partnership. (Spain)
SREA	Senior Real Estate Analyst
SRES	Senior Real Estate Specialist
SRF	Supplemental Reserve Facility. Established in 1997 to provide short-term assistance to countries experiencing exceptional balance of payments problems. (**IMF**)
SRG	Suriname, guilder (international currency symbol)
SRL	*Società a responsibilità limitata*. Limited company. (Italy)
SRO	self regulatory/regulating organization. US self regulatory organizations (i.e. the futures exchanges and National Futures Association) enforce minimum financial and sales practice requirements for their members.
SRP	suggested retail price
SRPA	Senior Real Property Appraiser
SSA	senior statistical assistant
SSA	Social Security Administration. US government agency responsible for maintaining and administering the Social Security programme.
SSA	standard spending assessment
SSAP	Statement of Standard Accounting Practice, *now* called **FRS** (Financial Reporting Standard). *See* Appendix 4.
SSC	small-saver certificate
SSE	Stockholm Stock Exchange. Stockholm Fondbors is the stock exchange of Sweden. The exchange is regulated by the Bank Inspection Board and the Riksbanker.
SSI	social security income
SSI	supplemental security income
SSNs	Situation Notices on the London Stock Exchange (**LSE**) which contain extensive details of a corporation action

SSP   statutory sick pay (UK)

SSTC   sold subject to contract

ST   stock transfer

STAGFLATION
stagnant (consumer demand) (price-wage) inflation. Stagnant economy marked by rising unemployment and spiralling inflation.

STAGS   Sterling Transferable Accruing Government Securities. British bonds backed by British Treasury securities.

STARFIRE   System to Accumulate or Retrieve Financial Information Random Extract

STD   São Tomé e Príncipe, dobra (international currency symbol)

Sté   *société*. Company. (France)

STER   sterling

ST EX   Stock Exchange

ST EXCH   Stock Exchange

STG   sterling

STI   Singapore Regional Training Institute (**IMF**)

STI   Straits Times Index (Singapore Stock Exchange)

STK   stock

STLG   sterling

STMS   short-term monetary support. Form of intervention mechanism in the **EU** under which the central bank of a country under exchange rate pressure due to balance of payments difficulties may borrow for a period, generally less than a year, from the central banks of other member countries.

STMT   statement

STO   standing order

STP   straight-through-processing

SUBSC   subscription

SUIT   Scottish and Universal Investment Trust

SUMI   Sumitomo Bank

SUNFED   Special United Nations Fund for Economic Development

SUP BEN   supplementary benefit

SUPERCAC
Screen-based electronic system operated by the principal stock exchange in France, the Paris Bourse

191

SUR	set-up reduction
SUR	Former Soviet Union ruble (currency)
S/V	surrender value (insurance)
SVA	statement of value added. Statement that shows how a company distributes the difference between sales revenue and the cost of materials and services it buys in order to generate that revenue.
SVC	El Salvador, colón (international currency symbol)
SVC	stored value card. Also called an electronic purse.
SVGS	savings
SWACHA	South Western Automated Clearing House Association (US)
SWIFT	Society for Worldwide Interbank Financial Telecommunications. Global dedicated computer network, based in Brussels, which provides a credit-transfer system between member banks, operated on a non-profit basis.
SWING	sterling warrant into gilt-edged stock. Authorized by the Bank of England in 1987, an option to buy or sell a specific gilt, then sold by an appointed dealer.
SWX	Swiss Exchange
SY CRS	sundry creditors
SYP	Syria, pound (international currency symbol)
SZL	Swaziland, lilangeni (international currency symbol)

T

T$	Tongan pa'anga divided into 100 seniti (currency)
TA	Travel/travelling allowance
TAA	tactical asset allocation
TAA	Trade Adjustment Assistance. TAA is a US policy authorized by the 1974 Trade Act to offer aid to workers laid off due to competition from imported goods. Such assistance includes job placement, instruction, and relocation support.
TACHA	Tennessee Automated Clearing House Association (US)
TAFE	technical and further education
TALISMAN	transfer accounting, lodgement for investors, stock management. Replaced by **CREST**.
TANs	tax anticipation notes
TAPOs	traded average price options. TAPO contracts are fundamentally insurance policies for the London Metal Exchange **(LME)**.
TAR	throughput accounting ratio
TARGET	Trans-European Automated Real-time Gross settlement Express Transfers system of Inter-bank payments. Introduced on 1 January 1999 to regulate transactions between commercial banks and the European Central Bank **(ECB)**.
TAURUS	Transfer and Automated Registration of Uncertified Stock. Paperless settlement system which was to have been introduced by the London International Stock Exchange in 1994, but was abandoned. Since then a new electronic share register **(CREST)** has been introduced.
TBA	to be advised/agreed/announced
TBF	Transferts Bank de France. Real-time gross settlement system.
T-BILL	treasury bill (US)
T-BOND	treasury bond (US)
TCA	Technician in Costing and Accounting. Institute of Cost and Executive Accountants.
TCGA	Taxation of Chargeable Gains Act (UK, 1992)
TCPA	Town and Country Planning Act/Association
TDA	tax-deferred annuity

TDI   taxpayer delinquent investigation. US term for routine follow-up on past-due tax and/or penalty matters.

TDR   treasury deposit receipt

TE   trade expenses

TECH   Technical Release put out by the Business Law Committee of the **ICAEW**.

TECHRICS

Technical Survey of the Royal Institution of Chartered Surveyors

TED   tenders electronic daily. Free database of **EU** tenders

TEM   *titulos de establizacion monetaria.* Monetary stablization notes. Securities issued by the central bank of Venezuela to absorb the excess lending capacity, stemming from oil revenues of the Venezuelan banking system.

TEP   traded endowment policy. Endowment policy (life assurance) which is sold in the open market before maturity.

TER   total expense ratio

TESSA   Tax-Exempt Special Savings Account. UK tax shelter savings plan open to all individuals aged 18 or over for money held in deposit in a bank or building society. Interest is not taxable provided no withdrawals are made during the five-year plan. The total sum invested could not exceed £9000, of which not more than £3000 could be deposited in the first 12 months. After five years investors could roll their investment into a second TESSA and continue contributions, if appropriate, up to the overall limit of £9000. TESSAs were replaced by Individual Savings Accounts (**ISA**s) in 1999.

TF   tax free

TGR   treasury investment growth receipt, zero coupon bonds issued by the Treasury

THB   Thailand, baht (international currency symbol)

THE   Technical Help for Exporters. Part of British Standards Institute (**BSI**)

THLRA   Taft-Hartley Labor Relations Act. Also know as Labor Management Relations Act, passed into law in 1947, provisions of which include injunctions against labour strikes.

TIA   Tax Institute of America

TIBOR   Tokyo Interbank Offered Rate. Japanese equivalent of **LIBOR**.

TIGR   Treasury Investment Growth Receipts (US)

TILA   Truth in Lending Act. Federal legislation enacted in 1968 that requires lenders to disclose to borrowers the true cost of loans and make interest rates and terms of loans simple to understand.

TIN	taxpayer identification number (US)
TJR	Tajikistan, rouble (international currency symbol)
TK	Bangladesh taka divided into 100 poisha (currency)
TL	Turkish lira divided into 100 kurus (currency)
TLF	transferable loan facility
TLO	total loss only (insurance)
TMM	Turkmenistan, manat (international currency symbol)
TMO	telegraphic money order
TMT	Technology, Media, and Telecommunications stocks. Used to cover any stock that is technology based.
TMWR	*Tax Management Weekly Report*. Reference publication from Bureau of National Affairs (BNA).
TND	Tunisia, dinar (international currency symbol)
T/O	turnover
TOB	terms of business
TOISA	Tessa Only Individual Savings Account
TOM	traded options market
TOO	to order only
TOP	Tonga, pa'anga (international currency symbol)
TOPIC	Teletext Output of Price Information by Computer
TOPIX	Share index of some 1200 stocks quoted on Japanese stock markets
TOS	temporarily out of stock
TP	*tout payé*. All paid. (France)
T&P	theft and pillage (insurance)
TPC	Transaction Processing Performance Council
TPI	tax and price index
TPS	Tax Payers' Society
TQM	total quality management. Business philosophy which aims that all employees of a firm have individual as well as a collective responsibility for maintaining high quality standards, in respect of both the products supplied by the firm and the attention paid to customer services and requirements.
TR	technical release
TRISACH	Tri-State Automated Clearing House Association (US)
TRL	Turkey, lira (international currency symbol)
TRN	trillion (one million million)

TRS	total return swaps
TS	tax shelter. Mechanism used by an investor to legally avoid or reduce tax liabilities.
TSA	The Securities Association. Formed in 1986 as a self-regulatory organization for securities dealing, by the amalgamation of the London Stock Exchange (**LSE**), now the International Stock Exchange, and the International Securities Regulatory Organization (**ISRO**), which then regulated dealers in **Eurobond**s and international equities in both registered and American depository receipt form. TSA merged with the Association of Futures Brokers and Dealers (**AFBD**) to form the Securities and Futures Authority in 1991.
TSB	Trustee Savings Bank. Originally established in Scotland in 1810 to encourage saving by people with low incomes. It grew to a large number of banks that were eventually amalgamated into a single enterprise. The TSB was floated on the stock exchange in 1986 and is now part of Lloyds TSB Bank.
tSO	The Stationery Office
TSO	trading standards officer
TSR	total shareholder return
TSRB	Top Salaries Review Body
TT	telegraphic transfer
TT$	Trinidad and Tobago dollar divided into 100 cents (currency)
TTD	Trinidad and Tobago, dollar (international currency symbol)
TTER	two-tier exchange rate
TTM	time to market
TUC	Trades Union Congress. UK organization that represents the collective interests of member trade unions in dealings with government and employers' organizations, and formulates general trade union policies.
TUM	Trades Union Movement
TUPE	Transfer of Undertakings (Protection of Employment) Regulations
TUUT	Trade Union Unit Trust
TV	terminal value
TVA	*taxe à valeur ajoutée*. Value-added tax, **VAT**. (France)
TWD	Taiwan, dollar (international currency symbol)
TX	tens of rupees
TZS	Tanzania, shilling (international currency symbol)

U

UA	Unit of Account (EU)
U/A	underwriting account
UAB	United Asian Bank
UAH	Ukraine, hryvnia (international currency symbol)
UAMCE	Union Africaine et Malgache de Coopération Économique. African and Malagasy Union for Economic Cooperation.
UB	United Bank (of Arizona)
UBAF	Union de Banques Arabes et Françaises. Union of Arab and French Banks.
UBB	Union Bank of Bavaria
UBI	United Business Investments
UBR	uniform business rate. Tax on business property that is the same percentage for the whole country. (UK)
UC	undercharge
UCAS	uniform cost accounting standards
UCB	United California Bank
UCITS	Undertaking for Collective Investments in Transferable Securities. EU directive which came into force in 1989 allowing unit trusts and open-ended investment companies to be traded throughout the EU.
UD	unfair dismissal
UDEAC	Union Douanière et Économique de l'Afrique Centrale. Central African Customs and Economic Union.
UDEAO	Union Douanière des États d'Afrique d'Ouest. Customs Union of West African States.
UEC	Union Européene des Experts Comptables Économique et Financiers. European Union of Accountants.
UEL	upper earning limit (UK, national insurance)
UEMOA	Union Économique et Monetaire Ouest Africaine. West African Monetary and Economic Union. Founded in 1994, the UEMOA aims to reinforce the competitiveness of the economic and financial activities of member states. Members are Benin, Burkina Faso, Côte d'Ivoire, Guinea–Bissau, Mali, Niger, Senegal, and Togo.

197

UFF	*ufficiale*. Official. (Italy)
UGS	Ugandan shilling (currency)
UGX	Uganda, shilling (international currency symbol)
UI	unemployment insurance (US)
U/I	unit of issue
UIB	United International Bank
UIP	uncovered interest party
UIT	unit investment trust
UITF	Urgent Issues Task Force (a sub-committee, established in 1991, of the Accounting Standards Board, **ASB**). Its function is to investigate matters needing urgent consideration. *See* Appendix 3.
UK£	United Kingdom pound (currency)
UKS	Uzbekistan soum (currency)
ULS	unsecured loan stock
UM	Ouguiya divided into five khoums (Mauritanian currency)
UN	United Nations
UNCDF	UN Capital Development Fund
UNCHS	UN Centre for Human Settlement. Also known as Habitat. UNCHS was founded in 1978 and assists over 600 million people living in health-threatening housing conditions.
UNCLOSE	UN Conference on the Law of the Sea
UNCTAD	UN Conference on Trade and Development. UNCTAD was established in 1964 to accelerate trade and economic development, particularly in developing countries. UNCTAD is the focal point within the UN system for the integrated treatment of development and interrelated issues in the area of trade, finance, technology investment and sustainable development.
UNDP	UN Development Programme. The UN Development Programme was established in 1965 and is the world's largest multilateral source of grants for sustainable human development. It coordinates most of the technical assistance provided by the UN system.
	UNDP's aims are: to help the UN become a powerful and cohesive force for sustainable human development; to focus its own resources on a series of objectives central to sustainable human development: poverty elimination, environmental regeneration, job creation, and advancement of women; to strengthen international cooperation for

sustainable human development; and serve as a major substantive resource on how to achieve this cooperation.

UNDP manages several associated funds. These include: UN Volunteer Programme (UNV); UN Development Fund for Women (UNIFEM); Office to Combat Desertification and Drought (UNSO); UN Capital Development Fund (UNCDF); UN Fund for Science and Technology for Development (UNFSTD); UN Revolving Fund for Natural Resources (UNRFNRE).

UNEP   UN Environment Programme. The UN Environment Programme was founded in 1972. Its mission is to provide leadership and encourage partnerships in caring for the environment by enabling nations and peoples to improve their quality of life without compromising that of future generations.

As the principal body in the field of the environment, its main functions are: analysing the state of the global environment; assessing environment trends; providing policy advice and early-warning information on environment threats; catalysing and promoting international cooperation and action; further development of international environment law, including interlinkages among conventions; advancing implementation of agreed international norms and policies and stimulating cooperative action to respond to emerging environmental challenges; coordinating environmental activities in the UN system; serving as an implementation agency of the Global Environment Facility; promoting environmental awareness and cooperation involving all sectors of society; serving as an effective link between the scientific community and policy makers; and providing policy and advisory services in key areas of institution-building to governments and institutions.

UNFPA   UN Fund for Population Activities. UNFPA was established in 1969, carries out development programmes in over 130 countries and territories, and is the largest international provider of population assistance to developing countries. In 1996 it provided support to 168 countries. The Fund's aims are to build up capacity to respond to needs in population and family planning; to promote awareness of population problems in both developed and developing countries and possible strategies to deal with them; and to assist developing countries at their request in dealing with population problems.

UNI   Union Network International. Europe-wide association of commerce and finance trade unions.

UNICE   Union of Industries of the European Communities (EU)

UNIDO   UN Industrial Development Organization. The UN Industrial Development Organization was established in 1966, becoming a specialized agency of the UN in 1985. Its mandate is to promote industrial development and cooperation and its activities are grouped into two main areas: (i) strengthening of industrial capacities; and (ii) cleaner and sustainable industrial development.

To support its services, UNIDO has engineers, economists, and technology and environmental specialists in Vienna, as well as professional staff in its network of Investment Promotion Service offices and field offices.

UNISON   Trade Union, amalgamation of National and Local Government Officers' Association, NALGO, National Union of Public Employees, NUPE, and Confederation of Health Service Employees, COHSE. (UK)

UNITAR   UN Institute for Training and Research. Established in 1965 to enhance the effectiveness of the UN in achieving its major objectives. Recently, its focus has shifted to training, with basic research being conducted only if extra-budgetary funds can be made available. Training is provided at various levels for personnel on assignments under the UN, its specialized agencies, or related organizations. By mid-2000 almost 47,000 participants from 200 countries had attended UNITAR courses, seminars, or workshops.

UNJSPB   UN Joint Staff Pension Board

UOB   United Overseas Bank

UPEFE   Union de la Presse Économique et Financière Européene. European Economic and Financial Press Union.

UPR   unearned premiums reserve. Fund set aside by an insurance company at the end of its financial year to cover risks to be borne in the future.

UPU   Universal Postal Union. UPU was established in 1875, when the Universal Postal Convention adopted by the Postal Congress of Berne on 9 October 1874 came into force. It has 189 member countries. The aim of the UPU is to assure the organization and perfection of the various postal services, and to promote the development of international collaboration in the field.

US$ United States dollar divided into 100 cents (*also* the currency of American Samoa, East Timor, Ecuador, Guam, Marshall Island, Fed. States of Micronesia, Northern Mariana Islands, Puerto Rico, Palau, Turks and Caicos Islands, British Virgin

Islands (£ sterling and EC$ also circulate), and US Virgin Islands)

USAID	United States Agency for International Development
USBS	United States Bureau of Standards. Federal government agency.
USCC	United States Chamber of Commerce. Federal government agency.
US CY	United States currency
USD	United States of America, dollar (international currency symbol)
USH	Ugandan shilling (currency)
USIF	United States Investment Fund
USM	Unlisted Securities Market. Established in 1980 to provide an easier route to the market for small or new companies. The market closed at the end of 1996, at which time USM companies could move either to the main market or the Alternative Investment Market (**AIM**).
USNB	United States National Bank
USSB	United States Savings Bond
USS & LL	United States Savings and Loan League
USTC	United States Tax Court
UTA	Unit Trust Association
UTR	unique taxpayer reference used by UK Inland Revenue
UUV	*unter üblichem Vorbehalt*. Errors and omissions excepted. (Germany)
U/W	underwriter
UYP	Uruguay, peso; *also* nuevo peso (currency)
UYU	Uruguay, peso (international currency symbol)
UZS	Uzbekistan, som (international currency symbol)

V

VA	value added
VA	value analysis
VA	voluntary arrangement
VAL	valuation
VAT	value-added tax. Indirect tax imposed by the government on the value added to goods or services.
VATTR	Value-Added Tax Tribunal
VC	variable cost
VC	venture capital. Source of financing for start-up companies and businesses undertaking major new developments.
VCT	Venture Capital Trust. Scheme for quoted companies to receive tax-free dividends and capital gains for pooled investments in qualifying unquoted trading companies. Principal requirement is that at least 70 per cent of investments must be in smaller companies either unquoted or on **AIM**.
VDT	visual display terminal
VDU	visual display unit
VEB	Venezuela, bolívar (international currency symbol)
VER	*Verein*. Association/Company. (Germany)
VFD	value for duty
VFM	value for money
VIBOR	Vienna interbank offered rate
Vier	*Viernes*. Association/Company. (Germany)
VIES	**VAT** information exchange system. Electronic system for national governments under the **IDA** programme. (EU)
VIF	variable import fee
VIRT-X	pan-European cross-border blue chip exchange with fully electronic trading
VITA	Volunteers In Tax Assistance
VJ	voluntary jurisdiction
VN$	Vietnamese dollar
VNB	Valley National Bank

VND   Vietnam, dong (international currency symbol)

VPC   *vente par correspondence*. Mail order. (France)

VRM   variable rate mortgage (US)

VRN   variable rate note

VSD   vendor's shipping document

VT   Vanuatu, vatu (international currency symbol)

VWAP volume weighted average price. Calculated by dividing the value of trades by the volume over a given period. A closing 10-minute VWAP is used to set closing prices on the order book.

W

W	South Korean won (currency)
WA	withholding agent (US)
WA£	West African pound
WAB	Wage Appeals Board
WAC	wage analysis and control
WACC	weighted average cost of capital
WACHA	Wisconsin Automated Clearing House Association (US)
WAM	walk-around money
WAM	wrap-around mortgage (US)
WAMA	West African Monetary Agency (Sierra Leone)
WAMU	West African Monetary Union
WB	World Bank. The World Bank Group consists of four institutions: the International Bank for Reconstruction and Development (**IBRD**), established in 1945; the International Finance Corporation (**IFC**), established in 1956; the International Development Association (**IDA**), established in 1960; and the Multilateral Investment Guarantee Agency (**MIGA**), established in 1988. The aim of all four institutions is to reduce poverty around the world by strengthening the economies of poor nations. (UN)
WC	working capital. Current assets minus current liabilities.
WCCU	World Council of Credit Unions
WCL	World Confederation of Labour. WCL was founded in 1920 as the International Federation of Christian Trade Unions, and went out of existence in 1940 as a large proportion of its 3.4 million members were in Italy and Germany, where affiliated unions were suppressed by the Fascist and Nazi regimes. Reconstituted in 1945 and declining to merge with the World Federation of Trade Union (**WFTU**) or International Confederation of Free Trade Unions (**ICFTU**), its policy was based on the papal encyclicals *Rerum novarum* (1891) and *Quadragesimo anno* (1931), and in 1968 it became the WCL and dropped its openly confessional approach.
W/D	withdrawal
WDA	Welsh Development Agency

WDA	writing-down allowance
WDV	written-down value
WEBS	World Equity Benchmark Series
WEIA	wife's earned income allowance
WES	World Economic Survey
WESTPAY	Western Payments Alliance
WFB	Wells Fargo Bank
WFP	World Food Programme. World's largest international food aid organization, which is dedicated to both emergency relief and development programmes.
WFTC	working families tax credit (UK)
WFTU	World Federation of Trade Unions. WFTU was founded in 1945 with the participation of all the trade union centres in the countries in the anti-Hitler coalition. The aim was to reunite the world trade union movement at the end of World War II. The acute political differences among affiliates, especially the east-west confrontation in Europe on ideological lines, led to a split. A number of affiliated organizations withdrew in 1949 and established the International Confederation of Free Trade Unions (**ICFTU**).
WGC	World Gold Council. Major gold producers established the council in 1987 to stimulate trade in gold.
WH	withholding
WHSLE	wholesale
WI	when issued
WIN	Whip Inflation Now
WIN	work incentive (US)
WINGS	warrants in negotiable government securities
WIP	Wage Insurance Program
WIP	work in progress. Calculation of the value of a contract not completed at the end of an accounting period.
WIPO	World Intellectual Property Organization. World Intellectual Property Organization was established in 1970. Its objectives are to promote the protection of intellectual property throughout the world through cooperation among member states and to ensure administrative cooperation among the intellectual property Unions established by the Paris and Berne Conventions to afford protection in the field of intellectual property. Intellectual property comprises two main branches: industrial property (inventions, trademarks, and

industrial designs) and copyright and neighbouring rights (literary, musical, artistic, photographic, and audiovisual works).

WLI	work load index
WMATA	Washington Metropolitan Area Transit Authority Bonds
WNDP	with no down payment
WNL	within normal limits
WO	written order
W/O	written off
WOG	with other goods
WOTAG	Women's Taxation Action Group
WP	wire payment (US)
WPC	war pensions committee
WPCC	Wage and Price Control Council
WPI	wholesale price index
WPT	windfall profit tax. Tax on profits resulting from a sudden event favourable to a particular company or industry.
WR	warehouse receipt
WRI	war risks insurance
WSJ	*Wall Street Journal*
WST	Samoan tala (currency)
WT	wealth tax
WT	weekly takings
WT	withholding tax
WTIS	World Trade Information Service
WTO	World Trade Organization. The WTO was established in Geneva in 1995. It replaced the General Agreement on Tariffs and Trade (**GATT**). The WTO is charged with the further development of and the policing of the multilateral trading system along the principles followed by the eight Rounds of Trade Negotiations concluded under its predecessor.
WTP	willing(ness) to pay
W/W	weight for weight
WWAP	worldwide asset position
Wz	*Warenzeichen*. Trademark. (Germany)

X

X	$10 bill (US)
XA	ex all
XAF	franc CFA. Communauté financière Africaine (**CFA**) franc (international currency symbol)
XAG	Silver, ounces (international currency symbol)
XAU	Gold, ounces (international currency symbol)
XB	ex bonus (without bonus shares)
XC	ex capitalization
XC	ex coupon
XCD	East Caribbean dollar (international currency symbol). The currency of St Kitts and Nevis, St Lucia, and St Vincent and the Grenadines.
XCL	excess current liabilities (insurance)
XCO	Crude oil barrels, XE.com Index (international currency symbol)
XCP	ex coupon
XD	ex-dividend. Without dividend. Purchase of a security quoted ex-dividend does not have the right to the next dividend when due; this belongs to the seller. *Also* XDIV.
XDR	International Monetary Fund (**IMF**) special drawing right (international currency symbol)
XETRA	Electronic order driven trading system
XETRA-DAX	
	Frankfurt stocks and shares index (Germany)
XI	ex interest
XN	ex new, without right to new shares
X-NOTE	US $10 note
XOF	Communauté financière Africaine franc. The currency of Benin, Burkina Faso, Guinea–Bissau, and Senegal.
XP	express paid
XPD	Palladium, ounces (international currency symbol)
XPF	franc CFP. Communauté financière du Pacifique (CFP) franc (international currency symbol). The currency of New Caledonia, French Polynesia, and Wallis and Futuna.

XPT

XPT	Platinum, ounces (international currency symbol)
XR	ex rights. *Also* XRTS.
XS	expenses
XW	ex warrants
XX-note	$20 bill (US)

Y

Y	Chinese yuan (currency)
¥	Japanese yen (currency)
Y2K	Year 2000. The "millennium bug" which was thought likely to cause havoc to computers and the financial world did not materialize.
YA	York Antwerp rules
YD	Yemeni dinar (currency)
YD	Yugoslav dinar (currency)
YER	yearly effective rate (of interest)
YER	Yemen, rial (international currency symbol)
YRls	Yemeni riyal (currency)
YTD	year to date
YUD	Yugoslavia, dinar (international currency symbol)

Z

Z$	Zimbabwe dollar divided into 100 cents (currency)
ZAI	*zaibutsu* (money clique). Plutocratic oligarchy of Japanese wealthy families such as the Mitsubishi, Mitsui, and Sumitomo.
ZAR	South Africa, rand (international currency symbol)
ZBA	zero balance account
ZBB	zero-based budgeting (US)
ZEG	zero economic growth
Zł	Polish złoty (currency)
ZMK	Zambia, kwacha (international currency symbol)
ZPG	zero population growth
ZRZ	Zaïre, *former* currency of Zaïre, *now* Democratic Republic of the Congo that uses Congo franc
ZWD	Zimbabwe, dollar (international currency symbol)

Appendix 1

MONETARY SYMBOLS

American Samoa	**US$**	United States dollar
Andorra	**€**	euro
Anguilla	**EC$**	East Caribbean dollar
Antigua and Barbuda	**EC$**	East Caribbean dollar
Ascension Island	**£**	St Helena pound
Australia	**$A**	Australian dollar
Austria	**€**	euro
Bahamas, The	**B$**	Bahamian dollar
Barbados	**BD$**	Barbados dollar
Belgium	**€**	euro
Belize	**BZ$**	Belize dollar
Bermuda	**Bd$**	Bermuda dollar
Brazil	**R$**	cruzeiro real
Brunei	**B$**	Brunei dollar
Canada	**C$**	Canadian dollar
Cayman Islands	**CI$**	Cayman Islands dollar
Chile	**Ch$**	peso
Colombia	**Col$**	peso
Cook Islands	**$NZ**	New Zealand dollar
Costa Rica	**¢**	Costa Rican colón
Cyprus	**£C**	Cyprus pound
Dominica	**EC$**	East Caribbean dollar
Dominican Republic	**RD$**	Dominican Republic peso
East Timor	**US$**	United States dollar
Ecuador	**US$**	United States dollar
Egypt	**£E**	Egyptian pound
El Salvador	**¢**	El Salvador colón
Fiji	**F$**	Fiji dollar
Finland	**€**	euro
France	**€**	euro

211

French Guiana	€	euro
Germany	€	euro
Ghana	¢	cedi
Greece	€	euro
Grenada	EC$	East Caribbean dollar
Guadeloupe	€	euro
Guam	US$	United States dollar
Guyana	G$	Guyana dollar
Hong Kong	HK$	Hong Kong dollar
Ireland	€	euro
Italy	€	euro
Jamaica	J$	Jamaican dollar
Japan	¥	yen
Kiribati	$A	Australian dollar
Kosovo	€	euro
Lebanon	£L	Lebanese pound
Liberia	L$	Liberian dollar
Luxembourg	€	euro
Marshall Islands	US$	United States dollar
Martinique	€	euro
Mayotte	€	euro
Mexico	Mex$	Mexican peso
Micronesia, Federated States of	US$	United States dollar
Monaco	€	euro
Montenegro	€	euro
Montserrat	EC$	East Caribbean dollar
Namibia	N$	Namibian dollar
Nauru	$A	Australian dollar
Netherlands	€	euro
New Zealand	$NZ	New Zealand dollar
Nicaragua	C$	córdoba
Nigeria	₦	naira
Niue	$NZ	New Zealand dollar
Norfolk island	$A	Australian dollar
Northern Mariana Islands	US$	United States dollar

Palau	US$	United States dollar
Paraguay	₲	guarani
Peru	S/.	nuevo sol
Philippines, The	₱	Philippine peso
Pitcairn Islands	$NZ	New Zealand dollar
Portugal	€	euro
Portuguese Azores	€	euro
Puerto Rico	US$	United States dollar
Réunion	€	euro
St Helena	£	St Helena pound
St Kitts and Nevis	EC$	East Caribbean dollar
St Lucia	EC$	East Caribbean dollar
St Pierre et Miquelon	€	euro
St Vincent and the Grenadines	EC$	East Caribbean dollar
Samoa	SA$	tala
San Marino	€	euro
Singapore	S$	Singapore dollar
Solomon Islands	SI$	Solomon Islands dollar
Spain	€	euro
Taiwan	NT$	new Taiwan dollar
Tokelau	$NZ	New Zealand dollar
Tonga	T$	pa'anga
Trinidad and Tobago	TT$	Trinidad & Tobago dollar
Tristan da Cunha	£	pound sterling
Turks and Caicos Islands	US$	United States dollar
Tuvalu	$T	Tuvalu dollar
United Kingdom	£	pound sterling
United States of America	$	United States dollar
Uruguay	Nur$	Uruguayan new peso
Vatican City State	€	euro
Virgin Islands, British	US$	United States dollar
Virgin Islands, US	US$	United States dollar
Zimbabwe	Z$	Zimbabwe dollar

Appendix 2

FINANCIAL REPORTING STANDARDS (FRSs)
(United Kingdom)

FRS 1   Cash flow statements

FRS 2   Accounting for subsidiary undertakings

FRS 3   Reporting financial performance

FRS 4   Capital instruments

FRS 5   Reporting the substance of transactions

FRS 6   Acquisitions and mergers

FRS 7   Fair values in acquisition accounting

FRS 8   Related party disclosures

FRS 9   Associates and joint ventures

FRS 10   Goodwill and intangible assets

FRS 11   Impairment of fixed assets and goodwill

FRS 12   Provisions, contingent liabilities and contingent assets

FRS 13   Derivatives and other financial instruments: disclosures

FRS 14   Earnings per share

FRS 15   Tangible fixed assets

FRS 16   Current tax

FRS 17   Retirement benefits

FRS 18   Accounting policies

FRS 19   Deferred tax

Appendix 3

URGENT ISSUES TASK FORCE (UITF)
(United Kingdom)

UITF Abstract 3	Treatment of goodwill on disposal of a business
UITF Abstract 4	Presentation of long-term debtors in current assets
UITF Abstract 5	Transfers from current assets to fixed assets
UITF Abstract 6	Accounting for post-retirement benefits other than pensions
UITF Abstract 7	True and fair view override disclosures
UITF Abstract 9	Accounting for operations in hyper-inflationary economies
UITF Abstract 10	Disclosure of directors' share options
UITF Abstract 11	Capital instruments: issuer call options
UITF Abstract 12	Lessee accounting for reverse premiums and similar incentives
UITF Abstract 13	Accounting for ESOP Trusts
UITF Abstract 14	Disclosure of changes in accounting policy
UITF Abstract 15	Disclosure of substantial acquisitions
UITF Abstract 16	Income and expenses subject to non-standard rates of tax
UITF Abstract 17	Employee share schemes
UITF Abstract 18	Pension costs following the 1997 tax changes in respect of dividend income
UITF Abstract 19	Tax on gains and losses on foreign currency borrowings that hedge an investment in a foreign enterprise
UITF Abstract 20	Year 2000 issues: accounting and disclosures
UITF Abstract 21	accounting issues arising from the proposed introduction of the euro
UITF Abstract 22	The acquisition of a Lloyd's business

Appendix 4

STATEMENTS OF STANDARD ACCOUNTING PRACTICE (SSAPs)
(United Kingdom)

SSAP 4   Accounting for government grants

SSAP 5   Accounting for VAT

SSAP 8   Treatment of taxation issued under the imputation system in the accounts of companies

SSAP 9   Stocks and long-term contracts

SSAP 13 Accounting for research and development

SSAP 17 Accounting for post balance sheet events

SSAP 19 Accounting for investment properties

SSAP 20 Foreign currency translation

SSAP 21 Accounting for leases and hire purchase contracts

SSAP 25 Segmental reporting

Appendix 5

STATEMENTS OF AUDITING STANDARDS (SASs)
(United Kingdom)

100 Objective and General Principles Governing an Audit of Financial Statements

110 Fraud and Error

120 Consideration of Law and Regulations

130 The Going Concern Basis in Financial Statements

140 Engagement Letters

150 Subsequent Events

160 Other Information in Documents Containing Audited Financial Statements

200 Planning

210 Knowledge of the Business

220 Materiality and the Audit

230 Working Papers

240 Quality Control for Audit Work

300 Accounting and Internal Control Systems and Audit Risk Assessments

400 Audit Evidence

410 Analytical Procedures

420 Audit of Accounting Estimates

430 Audit Sampling

440 Management Representations

450 Opening Balances and Comparatives

460 Related Parties

470 Overall View of Financial Statements

480 Service Organizations

500 Considering the Work of Internal Audit

510 The Relationship between Principal Auditors and other Auditors

520 Using the Work of An Expert

600 Auditors' Reports on Financial Statement

601 Imposed Limitation of Audit Scope

610 Reports to Directors or Management

620 The Auditors' Right and Duty to Report to Regulators in the Financial Sector

Appendix 6

FINANCIAL ACCOUNTING STANDARDS BOARD STATEMENT OF FINANCIAL ACCOUNTING STANDARDS (SFAS)
(United States of America)

SFAS 1 Disclosure of Foreign Currency Translation Information

SFAS 2 Accounting for Research and Development Costs

SFAS 3 Reporting Accounting Changes in Interim Financial Statements – an amendment of APB Opinion No. 28

SFAS 4 Reporting Gains and Losses from Extinguishment of Debt – an amendment of APB Opinion No. 30

SFAS 5 Accounting for Contingencies

SFAS 6 Classification of Short-Term Obligations Expected to Be Refinanced – an amendment of ARB No. 43, Chapter 3A

SFAS 7 Accounting and Reporting by Development Stage Enterprises

SFAS 8 Accounting for the Translation of Foreign Currency Transactions and Foreign Currency Financial Statements

SFAS 9 Accounting for Income Taxes: Oil and Gas Producing Companies – an amendment of APB Opinions No. 11 and 23

SFAS 10 Extension of "Grandfather" Provisions for Business Combinations – an amendment of APB Opinion No. 16

SFAS 11 Accounting for Contingencies: Transition Method – an amendment of FASB Statement No. 5

SFAS 12 Accounting for Certain Marketable Securities

SFAS 13 Accounting for Leases

SFAS 14 Financial Reporting for Segments of a Business Enterprise

SFAS 15 Accounting by Debtors and Creditors for Troubled Debt Restructurings

SFAS 16 Prior Period Adjustments

SFAS 17 Accounting for Leases: Initial Direct Costs – an amendment of FASB Statement No. 13

SFAS 18 Financial Reporting for Segments of a Business Enterprise: Interim Financial Statements – an amendment of FASB Statement No. 14

SFAS 19 Financial Accounting and Reporting by Oil and Gas Producing Companies

SFAS 20 Accounting for Forward Exchange Contracts – an amendment of FASB Statement No. 8

Appendix 6

SFAS 85 Yield Test for Determining whether a Convertible Security is a Common Stock Equivalent – an amendment of APB Opinion

SFAS 86 Accounting for the Costs of Computer Software to Be Sold, Leased, or Otherwise Marketed

SFAS 87 Employers' Accounting for Pensions

SFAS 88 Employers' Accounting for Settlements and Curtailments of Defined Benefit Pension Plans and for Termination Benefits

SFAS 89 Financial Reporting and Changing Prices

SFAS 90 Regulated Enterprises – Accounting for Abandonments and Disallowances of Plant Costs – an amendment of FASB Statement No. 71

SFAS 91 Accounting for Nonrefundable Fees and Costs Associated with Originating or Acquiring Loans and Initial Direct Costs of Leases – an amendment of FASB Statements no. 13, 60, and 65 and a rescission of FASB Statement No. 17

SFAS 92 Regulated Enterprises – Accounting for Phase-in Plans – an amendment of FASB Statement No. 71

SFAS 93 Recognition of Depreciation by Not-for-Profit Organizations

SFAS 94 Consolidation of All Majority-owned Subsidiaries – an amendment of ARB No. 51, with related amendments of APB Opinion No. 18 and ARB No. 43, Chapter 12

SFAS 95 Statement of Cash Flows

SFAS 96 Accounting for Income Taxes

SFAS 97 Accounting and Reporting by Insurance Enterprises for Certain Long-Duration Contracts and for Realized Gains and Losses from the Sale of Investments

SFAS 98 Accounting for Leases: Sale-Leaseback Transactions Involving Real Estate, Sales-Type Leases of Real Estate, Definition of the Lease Term, and Initial Direct Costs of Direct Financing Leases – an amendment of FASB Statements No. 13, 66, and 91 and a rescission of FASB Statement No. 26 and Technical Bulletin No. 79-11

SFAS 99 Deferral of the Effective Date of Recognition by Depreciation by Not-for-Profit Organizations – an amendment of FASB Statement No. 93

SFAS 100 Accounting for Income Taxes-Deferral of the Effective Date of FASB Statement No. 96 – an amendment of FASB Statement

SFAS 101 Regulated Enterprises – Accounting for the Discontinuation of Application of FASB Statement No. 71

SFAS 102 Statement of Cash Flows – Exemption of Certain Enterprises and Classification of Cash Flows from Certain Securities Acquired for Resale – an amendment of FASB Statement No. 95

SFAS 103 Accounting for Income Taxes-Deferral of the Effective Date of FASB Statement No. 96 – an amendment of FASB Statement

SFAS 104 Statement of Cash Flows-Net Reporting of Certain Cash Receipts and Cash Payments and Classification of Cash Flows from Hedging Transactions – an amendment of FASB Statement

SFAS 105 Disclosure of Information about Financial Instruments with Off-Balance-Sheet Risk and Financial Instruments with Concentrations of Credit Risk

SFAS 106 Employers' Accounting for Postretirement Benefits Other Than Pensions

SFAS 107 Disclosures about Fair Value of Financial Instruments

SFAS 108 Accounting for Income Taxes-Deferral of the Effective Date of FASB Statement No. 96 – an amendment of FASB Statement

SFAS 109 Accounting for Income Taxes

SFAS 110 Reporting by Defined Benefit Pension Plans of Investment Contracts – an amendment of FASB Statement No. 35

SFAS 111 Rescission of FASB Statement No. 32 and Technical Corrections

SFAS 112 Employers' Accounting for Postemployment Benefits – an amendment of FASB Statements No. 5 and 43

SFAS 113 Accounting and Reporting for Reinsurance of Short-Duration and Long-Duration Contracts

SFAS 114 Accounting by Creditors for Impairment of a Loan – an amendment of FASB Statements No. 5 and 15

SFAS 115 Accounting for Certain Investments in Debt and Equity Securities

SFAS 116 Accounting for Contributions Received and Contributions Made

SFAS 117 Financial Statements of Not-for-Profit Organizations

SFAS 118 Accounting by Creditors for Impairment of a Loan-Income Recognition and Disclosures – an amendment of FASB Statement No. 114

SFAS 119 Disclosure about Derivative Financial Instruments and Fair Value of Financial Instruments

SFAS 120 Accounting and Reporting by Mutual Life Insurance Enterprises and by Insurance Enterprises for Certain Long-Duration Participating Contracts – an amendment of FASB Statements No. 60, 97, and 113 and Interpretation No. 40

SFAS 121 Accounting for the Impairment of Long-Lived Assets and for Long-Lived Assets to Be Disposed Of

SFAS 122 Accounting for Mortgage Servicing Rights – an amendment of FASB Statement No. 65

Appendix 6

SFAS 123 Accounting for Stock-Based Compensation

SFAS 124 Accounting for Certain Investments Held by Not-for-Profits Organizations

SFAS 125 Accounting for Transfers and Servicing of Financial Assets and Extinguishments of Liabilities

SFAS 126 Exemption from Certain Required Disclosures about Financial Instruments for Certain Nonpublic Entities – an amendment to FASB Statement No. 107

SFAS 127 Deferral of the Effective Date of Certain Provisions of FASB Statement No. 125 – an amendment to FASB Statement No. 125

SFAS 128 Earnings per Share

SFAS 129 Disclosure of Information about Capital Structure

SFAS 130 Reporting Comprehensive Income

SFAS 131 Disclosures about Segments of an Enterprise and Related Information

SFAS 132 Employers' Disclosures about Pensions and Other Postretirement Benefits – an amendment of FASB Statements No. 87, 88, and 106

SFAS 133 Accounting for Derivative Instruments and Hedging Activities

SFAS 134 Accounting for Mortgage-Backed Securities Retained after the Securitization of Mortgage Loans Held for Sale by a Mortgage Banking Enterprise – an amendment of FASB Statement No. 65

SFAS 135 Rescission of FASB Statement No. 75 and Technical Corrections

SFAS 136 Transfers of Assets to a Not-for-Profit Organization or Charitable Trust That Raises or Holds Contributions for Others

SFAS 137 Accounting for Derivative Instruments and Hedging Activities – Deferral of the Effective Date of FASB Statement No. 133 – an amendment of FASB Statement No. 133

SFAS 138 Accounting for Certain Derivative Instruments and Certain Hedging Activities – an amendment of FASB Statement No. 133

SFAS 139 Rescission of FASB Statement No. 53 and amendments to FASB Statements No. 63, 89, and 121

SFAS 140 Accounting for Transfers and Servicing of Financial Assets and Extinguishments of Liabilities – a replacement of FASB Statement No. 125

SFAS 141 Business Combinations

SFAS 142 Goodwill and Other Intangible Assets

SFAS 143 Accounting for Asset Retirement Obligations

SFAS 144 Accounting for the Impairment or Disposal of Long-Lived Assets